DECISION INTELLIGENCE SELLING

TRANSFORM THE WAY YOUR PEOPLE SELL

ROY WHITTEN & SCOTT ROY

Niche Pressworks
INDIANAPOLIS, IN

Decision Intelligence Selling

ISBN: 978-1-952654-05-3 eBook
ISBN: 978-1-952654-06-0 Paperback
ISBN: 978-1-952654-07-7 Hardback

Library of Congress Control Number: 2020909712

Published by Niche Pressworks; NichePressworks.com

DEDICATION

*To the Strategic Leadership Team and Consultants
of Whitten & Roy Partnership
and to our clients throughout the world.*

*Your vision, collaboration, and commitment
have made all of this possible.*

TABLE OF CONTENTS

PART ONE

TRANSFORMATION, NOT IMPROVEMENT

CHAPTER 1

A NEW POSSIBILITY FOR AN OLD PROFESSION

"I've got fifteen sales reps and a manager. They're just running around, doing what they think is right, hoping to get lucky." Mark Campbell took another sip of beer and continued his story.[1]

"Nine months ago, the company hired me to manage their Public Sector vertical. We're a technology company, and we have three offerings: management consulting, systems integration, and managed services. I've dealt with this situation before. It's complicated, but it's not impossible to fix.

"I knew they were struggling, but I didn't know how bad it really was until I attended my first sales qualification meeting." He gave a short laugh and shook his head. "As part of learning

---

1   Mark Campbell has given permission to use his real name.

the business, I went along to this 'Go/No Go' meeting to learn their criteria for deciding which deals to pursue."

He swallowed more of his beer and grimaced as he set his glass on the oaken pub table around which we were sitting. "Our Head of Sales opened the discussion by introducing a potential deal from the Oracle channel. She gave a two-sentence pitch and said, 'I think we should go for it.' Four of the seven people sitting around the conference table said, 'Yeah, let's do it.' *And that was it!* The meeting was over in three minutes—no real discussion and no clear criteria!"

He was equally dismayed at the rest of the sales operation. "There was no system, no discipline, no consistent way of selling or approaching the customer—no common language, no shared process, and no ability to use the pipeline to accurately predict future sales. It was like, *let's just keep throwing mud at the wall and see what sticks.*"

He was an experienced sales professional. It was painful for him to watch what he called "an uncoordinated, undisciplined, thoroughly random approach to market." He admitted that, in the face of such chaos and as the "new boy on the block," he spent the next few months keeping his head down and focusing on the performance of his sector.

Things changed, however, when the CEO, fed up with the lack of sales performance, fired the Head of Sales and asked Mark to take her place. The job came with two clear objectives: land bigger deals and increase sales by 15%. And get it done within twelve months.

"Well, I'm an ambitious guy," Mark said with a smile, "and I like a challenge. So, I took the job." We paused to order another round. When the beer arrived, Mark carried on.

"That was two months ago. I spent the first thirty days uncovering even more crap than I already knew about. The three lines of business only vaguely cooperated with each other. We had no integrated offering for the market. I'd already seen the complete lack of process and discipline in the sales force. What I hadn't fully appreciated was the bad blood between several of the players that was affecting morale across the board.

"At *my* first Go/No Go meeting, I tried to introduce some process. I appealed to data and asked James, who was presenting an opportunity, for a written risk assessment. The deal had been poorly sold by the software rep who recommended our company as the systems integrator. It would require a significant amount of our resources to get it right, and this would eliminate resources for several other, more promising opportunities. James looked me straight in the eye and said, 'I've already discussed this with the CEO, and he's given his approval. Do you have a problem with that?' I wanted to punch his lights out. But this was my first meeting, so I swallowed my anger and asked him to bring me the risk assessment later that afternoon.

"Just before five o'clock, when there was little time for discussion, James knocked on my office door. He hadn't prepared the assessment, of course, and he brought a message from his buddy, the CEO: 'Do this deal.'

"I reached the CEO by phone—he had left early—and he confirmed that, yes, he had approved the deal with James. That's when I knew things had to change, or I was going to quit."

Mark shared a few more examples of the obstacles he was facing. "I want a salesforce that works together as a team, but I've got a bunch of *prima donnas* who keep undercutting each other to increase their personal paychecks. I want a sales process that we all follow, but I've got four *lone wolves* who refuse to follow a process, three *go-along-to-get-along* people who change direction when the wind blows, and everyone else trying to figure out how things really work around here.

"So," Mark concluded, "I've been looking for something to make this all work. Yes, we need a process, a selling system, but we need something *more*. I'm very familiar with all the major sales training programs. It's all good stuff, but I'm not *feeling the magic*. We need something that's going to really change people, pull them together as a team, and lift them out of the tension we're all in." He raised his glass in our direction. "And here I am talking to you when all I thought I'd be doing today was playing a little golf."

Six hours earlier, we had met by "the merest of chances," as Mark later put it. It was a Saturday morning, and we too had decided to get away for a round of golf. As we were preparing to tee off, Mark walked up with his bag and asked to join us. We introduced ourselves and pulled out our drivers. The weather was surprisingly warm for late fall in England, the greens were firm and dry, and our conversation was lighthearted and lively. As we were walking off the 18th green, Mark asked if we had time for a beer. That's what brought us to this conversation.

After his comment about wanting to *feel the magic,* we sat in silence for a while, watching the early sunset turn the dome of St. Paul's to bright orange. He added a few more details about why it was the right time to act: his position was secure, he had the authority to run sales the way he wanted, there were no rivals for his job, and he was respected by his colleagues. We suggested that the next step was to keep talking about the problems to be solved, and we agreed to visit him at work the following week.

That visit led to numerous meetings with Mark and his team, which resulted in our agreement to work together. His thoughtful leadership got us off to a good start. He planned carefully about whom to involve and how to do it. We developed a schedule of activity to prepare people for a training experience that promised to be unusual and intriguing.

We conducted the training in the conference room of the golf club where we had first met Mark. From the balcony of the clubhouse, the view of greater London, from Wembley Arch to Canary Wharf, made it easy to pull ourselves "out of the weeds," as Mark put it, and to think big. The three-day experience was everything the three of us had hoped for.

The following week, we debriefed the training over a relaxed meal and some good wine. Mark started the conversation. "Usually, when a company sets up a sales training, you're given a schedule, you show up, the course happens, you have too much coffee and biscuits, and then everyone leaves. *This* was different. Before we met, you put us through a professional workstyle assessment and interviewed every participant. By the time the training happened, everyone was bought-in."

Who's proud of being called a salesman?

He continued. "The first morning, you asked a surprising question: 'Who's proud of being called a salesman?' We had a number of pure salespeople in the room, but *no one* put their hand up. You then deconstructed what sales was really about. You made the case that great selling was an honorable enterprise. At the coffee break, I heard people saying that selling *was* something they could feel good about, and they *wanted* to feel good about it. That was…*amazing*."

He nodded slowly before continuing. "The second big surprise was what I've since been calling the *Jedi mind trick*, that technique for getting focused in the present moment. Frankly, I was a skeptic. I thought it was mumbo jumbo, a bit of snake oil, just too different. But the rest of the room were ahead of me; they were really into it. My newest salesperson said, 'Come on, Mark, it's about being in the moment, getting your brain into what's happening…give it a go.'

"And the next morning, another person—a rather good snooker player who had left the training the previous evening and played in a championship—shared how he had used it to calm his nerves and sharpen his play."

> "You can have all the brainpower and all the skills in the world, but if your attitude sucks, you're going nowhere."

He thought some more. "The selling system itself was absolutely the right thing at the right time for us. And the importance of attitude, managing your own mindset as you work—that's the whole thing, isn't it? You can have all the brainpower and all the skills in the world, but if your attitude sucks, you're going nowhere."

That dinner launched the embedding process that follows our classroom trainings.[2] Mark wisely insisted on a program lasting several months, because, in his words, "No matter how

---

2   We have found that every classroom experience requires significant follow-up support if participants are to successfully apply what they have learned.

good the training, it's like having a tasting menu for dinner— interesting at the time, but the next day you can't remember what you ate." Over the following months, we designed and kept adapting an array of face-to-face refreshers—remote seminars, deal reviews, and individual coaching—to help his salespeople apply the practices they had learned.

Progress was steady, sometimes spectacular. There were a few failures along the way, from which people learned valuable lessons. Two salespeople quit rather than face up to their need for development, and another was fired. All three were replaced by people who had been hired because of their willingness and enthusiasm to *learn the way the company was now selling.* Each of them quickly grew into their roles.

The project lasted for six months. Soon after it ended, we met for a long, celebratory meal that gave us lots of time to look back on what we had accomplished and what we had learned. We recalled that Saturday morning when *the merest of chances* had brought us together. We told Mark how impressed we had been with the way he openly discussed the challenges he was facing and then asked for our opinion about what he might not be seeing.

"As a salesperson myself," he said, "I'm used to approaching clients who are determined to look like they know everything, who won't have anything put over on them, who are trying to control the conversation and shape *my* perspective. I'm humble enough to realize that there's a lot I don't know, and I didn't want to be a typical client for you. I decided to just lay all the sh*t right on you and see if you could help me figure it out. And you *really* listened.

"Furthermore, when we finished that first conversation, you didn't go for the jugular. You didn't shove anything at me or try to sell me something. You just said, 'Let's talk some more about what's going on.' I remember going home and telling my wife, 'I like these guys! I think they may be able to help me. They actually *want* to understand my business.'"

We then discussed what hadn't gone according to plan. "My biggest regret," said Mark, "is that I don't think we committed properly from the top of the organization. It wasn't like there was active obstruction. But we just missed opportunity after opportunity to exert top-level leadership and extend the way we were now being with *customers* to become the way *we* worked together as a company. *That* would have changed everything."

He shook his head and stayed silent for a moment. Obviously, this had been an ongoing disappointment.

"How did you handle that?" we asked.

He smiled. "I managed my attitude every day, just like you showed me."

And then, an even bigger smile. "It helped that our sales kept improving at every level throughout the year. We landed our biggest contract in the history of the company. We landed deals more quickly and for larger amounts than ever before. And we had an overall increase in sales of 30% during the year. *That* eased the pain a bit."

He leaned back in his chair, took a sip of wine, looked into the distance, and said, "But the *best* thing was providing the tools that people could use to turn themselves into really effective salespeople. It goes back to what I shared with you after that first round of golf. I know selling systems, and there are a lot of good ones. But I didn't just want a system; I wanted something that would change people for good. I didn't want my people to just follow a recipe. I wanted them to become great chefs."

> "I didn't want my people to just follow a recipe. I wanted them to become great chefs."

We spent a moment together in silence before Mark continued. "*I* didn't do the selling last year, *they* did. I just put the ingredients on the table and, with your help, taught them how to find their own brilliance and cook great meals. I helped them achieve a level of professionalism that they will have for the rest of their lives, no matter where they go or what they do. *That's* what I'm proudest of."

His voice raised a little, and he leaned forward. "You remember Hannah? Just before she left, we were talking, and she said, 'Wouldn't it be something to apply this to an entire company, not just sales?' And now, with your consultation, she's doing exactly that. I find that *really* pleasing—just knowing that what I helped happen has had a lasting impact."

And then Mark shared something personal. He told us about the Trans-Britain Race he had spent the year preparing to run—a celebration of his 50th birthday and, he admitted, an attempt to deny he was getting older. Despite a previous personal best of only seven miles, he'd committed to running a staggering six marathons in six consecutive days—up and down the hills of northern England and his native Scotland. When we started our project with his sales force, he started training for this challenge.

"After training for a few months, I was scared stiff about what I'd committed to do. I had too big an ego to drop out, but I was really scared that I wasn't going to finish—or worse, that I would damage myself."

He turned to Scott. "And then, during one of our coaching sessions, you reminded me of the 'Jedi mind trick,' which I *was* using in my sales management—but it just hadn't occurred to me to apply it to my personal life. You showed me how to use it to coach myself through the physical training and the race itself. It made all the difference. I not only completed the training; I actually finished the race. I was exhausted, but I wasn't damaged!

"Now, in my career, I'm understanding the way to *really change* business behavior.[3] It's not just systems and processes. You need them, and they've got to be right—but alone they won't make the permanent change that's needed. Neither will telling people what to do. What's needed is getting people to really understand *how* to develop and use their capabilities in the most powerful way. And executives and managers must learn how to coach them to do this."

He raised his glass in our direction.

"That's what you showed us—showed me—how to do. You gave us a workbook, but it was just an *aide-memoire*. What

---

3   After Mark left the company, he became Managing Director for the European division of a multinational human resources company. There, he *did* provide the "leadership from the top" that supported his head of sales to make our work with them a success. Now, he is an independent contractor and a consultant to numerous enterprises.

actually transformed us was the attitude shift that we learned to make, and keep making, each day at work. It changed the way we looked at clients, at sales opportunities, and at each other. You showed us how to coach ourselves, and now we can take it forward."

He finished with some advice for other sales leaders who wanted more from their sales force. "I would tell them this: if you think something can transform your business, *commit to it*. If you don't think it can, then don't bother. *Just don't do it halfway.*"

It's been nearly a decade since that chance meeting with Mark Campbell. During that time, we've conducted 300 projects with over 100 clients in 36 countries—large companies and small, B2B and B2C channels, complex selling as well as transactional, in both the "developed" and "developing" worlds. We've seen the remarkable benefits of applying transformational learning to the practice of sales. The journey has been rewarding, but it's not been easy or smooth.

The two of us also met by chance in 1986. Scott attended the transformational training program that Roy had co-founded, and he applied what he learned about mindset to the insurance business he had co-founded. Twenty years later, after a significant amount of individual success, we had become independent consultants. We were asked to collaborate on the design of a sales academy for a large high-street bank in the UK.

This bank maintained 1,100 branches and employed thousands of people throughout the UK. The work was so professionally successful and personally fulfilling that, in the spring of 2009, when the recession was at its height and the bank project was coming to an end, we decided to go into business together. We still have the receipt from our March 27th visit to the Thameside Pub, where, over a glass of real ale, we decided to create a partnership in which we would do exactly what we wanted to do with the clients we wanted to serve. We had worked for a full year to integrate our decades of experience into an effective approach to *transforming* sales. We suspected that we had something unique to offer, even during a recession.

We soon landed our first client. Our second and third clients followed in short order. We were pretty proud of ourselves, and we were doing some very good work. We had blended our expertise—Roy's experience with managing mindset and Scott's mastery of sales team development—and created an integrated training program that really worked for our clients in both the developed and developing worlds. Then, we hit a surprising bump in the road.

We had made it a priority to only work with clients we respected and liked. We could afford that luxury because there were only two of us, and we had self-funded the new business. However, eighteen months into our enterprise, we were making zero profit on client number one, and clients number two and three inexplicably (to us) refused to sign large contracts for continued work *despite* significant success in our early programs with them. We had signed client number four, and the work was going well, but we had to admit that although our sales consulting was working for our clients, the *way we were selling our consulting services* wasn't working for us. That was a bitter and ironic pill to swallow.

So, we took the time to take our medicine. We hit the pause button on our sales activity. We tore apart our selling system and generated an approach that represented a significant break from the past and charted a new path for the future. It took a few weeks, and just when we thought we had something that would work, *another* Mark—Mark Jopling—called. "I've got a new job," he said. "I want to see if you can help me with my new team."[4]

Two days later, armed with blank notebooks and determined to apply the new selling practice we had just developed, we took our seats at a conference table with Mark and his head of L&D. "I want my people to learn how to sell strategically," he said, "and I've set aside two hours for you to tell me how you would do that." This was the first test of our new approach. Before, we would have launched into a pitch. Now, we did something different.

"Well," we said, "the term 'strategically' is used in several different ways. Tell us what you mean by it and what you want them to do that they're not already doing." Mark sat up straighter, looking surprised. And then, he started talking about the way his sales reps conducted themselves with clients. He wanted them to listen more and pitch less, to quit jumping at the first possible product sale that came into their minds, to dig more deeply for client needs, and to be more involved with customers in developing potential solutions.

---

4   Mark Jopling has given permission to use his real name. He was a member of our third client's senior team before being promoted to this position.

We were well over an hour into the conversation—taking notes, helping him clarify his thinking—when suddenly he sat up straight, placed both hands on the conference table, and said, "*Now* I know what I want! I want our salespeople to sell to our clients the way you're selling to me!"

> "I want our salespeople to sell to our clients the way you're selling to me!"

Weeks later, when we were all together in the training room with his senior team, we shared this story to illustrate the need to help clients understand their problems before proposing solutions. Mark smiled and said, "Let me tell you the rest of the story. You were the sixth training company I'd interviewed that week. I gave each group two hours, and I started each conversation with the same invitation to 'tell us how you can help us.' You were the *only* supplier who *didn't* spend the entire two hours trying to pitch and convince me with a PowerPoint presentation. Instead, you opened up your notebooks and helped me explore what I really needed to build the team and increase our collective impact with customers."

He paused a minute to make sure his team was listening. "It was at *that moment* that I decided to hire you." We'll forever be grateful to Mark—certainly for hiring us, but even more for his openness about what it takes to inspire a client's trust. Up to that moment, we had a *theory* called Decision Intelligence Selling. After that moment, we had a confirmed *way* of selling that changed everything for us and for the like-minded sales leaders we've worked with since.

We are assuming that you are just such a leader. We have written this book for you. Our goal is to share enough real stories, insights, and transformational practices that you and the other key leaders in your business can immediately take your most effective steps to launch the type of sales transformation both Marks (Campbell and Jopling) engineered. This transformation is an art as well as a science. Making it happen is complex but not complicated. And it's *not* a mystery.

The path is logical and straightforward. But, as with all things genuinely transformational, it will challenge and keep challenging everything that has become *business as usual*— the mindset, systems, policies, and behaviors that sooner or later constrain every organization.

If you are one of those sales leaders searching for more than simply hitting a target, you're reading the right book. Perhaps, like the two leaders whose stories we've shared, you believe it's time to transform the *way* you and your people sell.

Let's go to work.

CHAPTER 2

A SPOTLIGHT ON SALES

A WAKE-UP CALL FOR BUSINESS

Mark Campbell was ahead of the sales leadership curve. He wanted a new way of doing business that was driven by a new way of selling. It was years later, on August 19, 2019, that corporate America appeared to wake up to what Mark had been seeing.

On that date, the Business Roundtable, a gathering of 181 CEOs representing the USA's largest corporations, produced a revolutionary document.[i] For forty years, the Roundtable had issued annual commentaries on the principles of business. On this date, they presented a statement that superseded their previous observations in order to offer a "modern standard for corporate responsibility."

They began their *Statement on the Purpose of a Corporation* by confirming their faith in the way nearly every business operates.

[People] deserve an economy that allows each person to succeed through hard work and creativity and to lead a life of meaning and dignity. We believe the free-market system is the best means of generating good jobs, a strong and sustainable economy, innovation, a healthy environment, and economic opportunity for all.

Then, they dropped a bombshell. They pledged to lead their companies according to five purposes, *in this order of priority*:

1. Delivering value to our customers.
2. Investing in our employees...compensating them fairly and providing important benefits...training and education that help[s] develop new skills for a rapidly changing world...foster[ing] diversity and inclusion, dignity and respect.
3. Dealing fairly and ethically with our suppliers.
4. Supporting the communities in which we work.
5. Generating long-term value for shareholders, who provide the capital.

The purpose that had driven business for decades, and which they had previously supported—namely, short-term profit for investors and shareholders—*doesn't even appear on the list. Long-*term profitability replaces this purpose, *and* it is in fifth place.

The bombshell, however, didn't explode. A few journalists hailed the statement as a long-awaited breakthrough in corporate thinking. Others regarded it as a cynical attempt to blunt anti-capitalist criticism. The press release was news for a couple of days, and then it dropped off the media's radar. Mostly, people didn't seem to know what to do with it.

Who knows? Maybe the 181 CEOs don't know what to do with it either.[ii]

SELLING IS THE KEY

The Business Roundtable highlighted a problem that is not easy to solve: How *do* you re-purpose your business around the well-being of everyone whose lives you impact *without* losing profitability?

Profit is critical. Without it, a business collapses—later, if not sooner. If you're too big to fail, your business won't actually die; it will just flop around like a beached whale while employees, clients, and communities suffer the consequences.

> How *do* you re-purpose your business around the well-being of everyone whose lives you impact *without* losing profitability?

Furthermore, having to generate a profit brings a far greater benefit than ensuring your company's survival. It requires that you deal with *reality*—with clients, employees, and the market—and rise to those challenges in a way that produces insight, innovation, and, more often than not, profound satisfaction for everyone involved. Ultimately, it requires individuals, teams of people, and entire companies to develop into better versions of themselves.

Profit itself is not the enemy. The real enemy is more insidious, showing its face slowly over time. It's the *belief* that pursuing profit will (someday) allow a company to address all of the *other* things that make a business worth being a part of. It's this belief that causes short-term profitability to become the *primary* star around which all business decisions orbit.

When that happens, you invite consequences that will actually compromise other things that are vital to your business: your relationship with clients and suppliers and the well-being of your employees and the communities in which you operate. Neglect these things long enough, and you wind up with a business that has little going for it *except* profitability.

> Neglect these things long enough, and you wind up with a business that has little going for it *except* profitability.

These 181 CEOs appear to be saying that they don't *want* to lead companies that continue to miss the point in this way. That certainly has been the case for all of the company leaders we've worked with. It may be the case for you as well.

Once you realize that this is a problem you want to solve, there's only one question that really matters: *Yes, but how?* How do you find the right relationship between profitability and the well-being of everyone affected by your enterprise? Which part of your business do you look at first? How do you diagnose what's wrong and develop a solution that actually solves the problem? How do you maintain financial viability as you do all this?

There's a very direct way to address these questions. It starts by acknowledging the obvious: your business serves your clients. Without clients, you don't have a business. And without client *loyalty*, you won't have a business that lasts.

There is credible research[iii] that identifies *the* business activity that creates or destroys client loyalty. It's not your marketing.

It's not who they know within your company. It's not even the quality and pace of your delivery. It's the way they are treated, regarded, and cared for *during the selling process*. It is *that* experience for which they are willing to pay more, buy more, forgive more, and refer more buyers to you.

Therefore, if you want to create a business that not only survives but thrives, take a penetrating look at the way your business *sells*. Not the way you *talk* about doing it, but the way it *actually* happens. The way your salespeople are with clients. The way your sales managers are with their teams. The way your systems, processes, and policies affect your entire sales force. With apologies to the King James Bible, you could go so far as to say, *"As you sell, so shall you reap."*

The sales leaders with whom we work know there are only two levers to pull to create profitability: decrease expenses and increase revenue. They also know that, while you can't cost-cut your way to growth, you can *sell* your way to it. And the *way* that you sell can reap benefits that exceed the financial return.

This was the insight Mark Campbell and his colleague shared: *"Imagine running an entire company in the way we're now selling to our clients. Wouldn't that be something?"*

Sales is both a window and a door. A window through which you can see the convictions, the behaviors, and the processes that are failing to match your vision and mission. A door through which you can successfully pass into a new way of being with clients and colleagues, a way that changes everything for good.

But the question remains: *how* do we do that?

If, like Mark, you are familiar with the many sales training programs on the market, you will know that a lot of them are thoughtful, well-researched, and technically sound. But, if you've attempted to use *any* training program with your sales force, it won't surprise you that research shows up to 87% of what sales-people learn in the classroom disappears from their practice within one month after returning to the field.[iv] *One month.*

Charting a new direction for sales requires your people to make personal and professional changes. Merely *improving* things isn't enough. You need a *transformation*.

TRANSFORMATION IS THE PATH

The word *transformation* has become popular in business circles. Unfortunately, as popularity rises, the power of a fresh word diminishes with overuse. We knew that *transformation* had eclipsed its expiration date when one of our clients referred to a 30% reduction in sales staff as "cost transformation."

> Merely *improving* things isn't enough. You need a *transformation*.

Let's explore for a moment what the word *really* means. Then, we can address how to do it.

We first encountered the concept of transformation during the 1960s when it was applied to personal development in what has become known as the Human Potential Movement. It described a radical shift in human thought and behavior—a profound and permanent change from the norm.

In the late 1990s, Transformative Learning became its own field of study.[v] Today, it draws on a wide range of thought and practice: from ancient wisdom to modern neuroscience. It focuses on *how* human beings undergo fundamental, permanent change—as individuals, in groups, and in institutions. It offers a unique understanding of why sales training doesn't stick, and it provides effective practices for helping people make the shifts in thought and action that can change selling—and the people who do it—for good.

Our clients utilize a simple formula, R=A+C+E™, to create the conditions in which transformation can occur (see Figure 2.1).[5] It involves requiring your sales force to develop themselves by addressing four fundamental elements in a way that is simple, practical, and integrated:

> **Transformation is about *getting results* and getting them in a way that people are proud of and *want* to keep doing.**

- **Results.** The sales results that they're seeking. Transformation is about *getting results* and getting them in a way that people are proud of and *want* to keep doing.
- **Attitude.** Noticing their state of mind as they work—whether or not they are really *committing* to what they're doing, taking full responsibility for their targets, and generating new opportunities. Knowing how to maintain a mindset that gives them greater access to their natural brilliance, boldness, and ingenuity.
- **Competence.** Mastering the art of having conversations that result in right action: selling conversations that engage clients, build trust, and generate committed action; sales management conversations that keep everyone thinking deeply, collaborating fully, and developing their expertise.

---

5   In 1986, Scott attended a training program co-founded by Roy. Afterwards he created this formula for use in his own business. Now, it is the framework that guides us in both our client delivery and the running of our own company.

- **Execution.** Doing the right thing at the right time with the right people. Developing and implementing a sales and management system that actually works—and that people actually want to do.

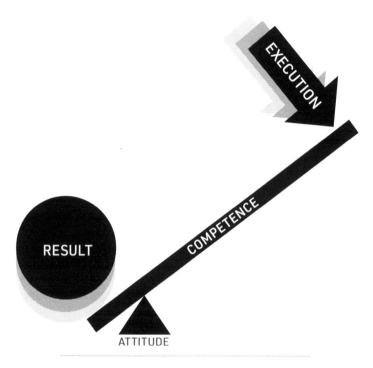

Figure 2.1 R=A+C+E™ — A Transformational Formula

When you successfully address all four of these elements, you experience two fundamental transformations that empower you to sell in a way that genuinely promotes the well-being of everyone involved *and* increases revenue and profitability.

First, you transform the *way* you sell. The next section of this book (Part Two) walks you through how to do this.

- **Chapter Three** explains the fundamental challenge to be faced: the core convictions about selling and managing salespeople that *everybody knows* are true—only they're not.
- **Chapter Four** introduces Decision Intelligence Selling—a framework sales teams use to build trust by leading their clients to make the best possible buying decisions.

Second, you transform the *people* who do the selling—to free them to adopt new practices and to keep themselves from defaulting to old behavior when the pressure is on. As Mark Campbell discovered, you can't just *tell* people to do things in a new way. You've got to provide an *experience* in which they find themselves *wanting* to do what the business *needs* them to do.

Part Three shows you how to apply R=A+C+E to develop your sales force in this way.

- **Chapter Five** illustrates the very human problem R=A+C+E addresses. It describes *autopilot*, a way of living and working that we all fell into around the age of five. It's why people have so much difficulty shifting their behavior and why developing new habits isn't necessarily such a good thing.
- **Chapter Six** focuses on the "R" in the formula, *Results.* It reveals the value of, and the practical steps involved in, cultivating what traditionally has been called *Deep Desire.* It's a way to aim your brain and generate what we refer to as your *natural brilliance.* We share the

neuroscience behind this development of the insight, boldness, and creativity we all had as children—and which we need to recover as adults.

- **Chapter Seven** concentrates on the "A," *Attitude.* It introduces Split Attention, a simple technique for immediately moving into present-moment awareness. It's at the heart of all our transformational practices, and it generates the wisdom, the passion, and the courage to make everything else work. This chapter introduces the ability to manage your own mindset moment-by-moment as you work—an immediate path to peak performance.

- **Chapter Eight** addresses "C," *Competence,* by introducing CLEAR™: a way to engage people—clients, colleagues, direct reports—that generates genuine trust, clear understanding, and committed action. Mastering this conversational skill allows sellers to lead clients to a decision and managers to develop the sales capability of their teams.

- **Chapter Nine** unpacks "E," *Execution.* It lays out the steps to execute Decision Intelligence Selling and get the results you seek. It explains how to design a simple system that eliminates wasted effort and unnecessary distractions for sellers and managers. It illustrates how to create the conditions that require and support your sales force to focus on the right activities, maintain an effective mindset, and *continue* to develop their skills as they work.

- **The last chapter**, Very Next Steps, is exactly what it says. It will get you started without overloading your circuits.

Two Final Comments:

You'll notice the word *we* throughout the book when normally an author would use *I*. We use it because we've written this book the way we developed our business. One of us thinks of something first, we discuss it in depth, and the end result is a joint creation, something that neither of us would have developed on our own. So, unless it's critical to the story, or just too inaccurate to attribute a thought or an action to both of us, we will be using *we* throughout the book.

You'll also notice that some of the people whose stories we share have given permission to use their real names (and in one case, a company name). In all the other cases, in order to preserve confidentiality, the stories are real, but the names are not.

Executive Summary

Businesses large and small are responding to a market calling for more enlightened operations that support the well-being of everyone involved *in addition* to generating profit for stake-holders. Leaders can make the changes required by focusing on the greatest engine of business growth—sales—and applying the insight and practical skills of transformational science.

You transform the *way you sell* by designing your version of Decision Intelligence (DQ) Selling. And you transform the *people who sell* by creating conditions that both require and empower people to sell this way—conditions that address the results they pursue and the attitude, competence, and execution with which they pursue it.

PART TWO

TRANSFORMING THE WAY YOU SELL

CHAPTER 3

LOCKED IN PLACE

"We have an executive who we've fast-tracked for promotion. He's spent his career in finance, and we've just given him a new job as managing director for a £500M division that, frankly, isn't doing very well. We were thinking of sending him for a week of crash sales management training at The Kellogg School of Management, but we want to offer him an alternative, and I thought of you guys. I know you train sales forces. Do you mentor sales executives?"

The caller was an HR manager for a British multinational telecom company. We had met her socially at an Italian restaurant in Crystal Palace, close to our homes in south London. It was the summer of 2011, and we hadn't actually mentored anyone yet, but it seemed like a great opportunity. It turned out to be exactly that.

EYES TO SEE AND EARS TO HEAR

The next day, Colin Annette[6] joined us on a conference call. He introduced himself by saying, "Look, I don't know anything about sales. I'm a finance nerd and have been for 20 years. I know numbers, and I know data. Sales, on the other hand, is a *black box. Nobody* knows how it works. Believe me, I've asked at least five colleagues to explain it to me."

> "Sales, on the other hand, is a black box. *Nobody* knows how it works."

"And…?"

"I learned three things: One, if you have to ask, you'll never know. Two, they may be good at it, but they can't explain it. Three, even if they could explain it, it would take more time than they've got to walk me through it."

After agreeing to work together, we asked him to go get some data—to follow his people around, watch what they do, and ask them why they're doing it. We asked him to describe the processes and systems they *actually* use and find out if they think they're effective *and* if they enjoy using them. And we scheduled a meal to review what he found.

Two weeks later, Colin walked into the restaurant with a thick file folder. We ordered our meal, and he laid onto the table several sheets of neatly printed graphs, columns of numbers, and some hand-drawn diagrams.

"Let's start with the salespeople," he said. "They're struggling, but, of course, that's why my predecessor is gone." He gave a slight smile and continued by describing the day he had spent

---

6   Colin Annette has generously given permission to use his real name.

with Jennifer, a senior sales rep with seven years of experience. He had planned to observe four people that day, but after two hours with Jennifer, he knew that plan was doomed.

"It was her *preparation* that screwed up my schedule. She set a two o'clock appointment with a client and then spent *four hours* searching the internet for company information, preparing value propositions, and assembling three slide decks to showcase the products she thought would catch the client's interest."

He acknowledged Jennifer's dilemma—the company's sales software *required* this level of preparation before an initial client visit—but he suspected that this was a waste of her time. "I thought our finance processes were over-the-top," he said, "but *this* was crazy. The program wouldn't let her skip through any screens. She had to complete each step—research, proposition development, risk assessment, and pricing—before getting electronic permission to proceed."

He tried to brush aside his opinion, repeating his refrain, "I don't know sales." We suggested that he trust his analytical experience and just give his opinion as to what was working and what wasn't.

"Wouldn't she be better off just sitting down with the client and *asking them* what they need?"

He stayed silent as he examined a few more sheets of paper. Finally, he said, "That preparation process doesn't survive a cost/benefit analysis. Wouldn't she be better off just sitting down with the client and *asking them* what they need?"

After that, the conversation picked up the pace. Colin was indeed an accomplished analyst. Together, we examined the data he'd gathered about Jennifer and the other four sales reps he'd observed, and we mapped what his sales team *actually did* to sell the company's products and services. We examined the entire system: target-setting, sales activity, tracking and reporting, and all of the management these things required.

> **It was a picture of dysfunction, but it was a *system*—it *kept itself going* even when it didn't produce the sales results the company was seeking.**

It was a picture of dysfunction—chaotic, self-limiting, and ineffective—but it was a *system*. One thing led to another, and—this is critical to understanding systems—it *kept itself going even when it didn't produce the sales results the company was seeking.*

This systemic perspective energized Colin. He had brought different colored pens, and he drew red stars where intervention was needed to take the system in a new direction.

"Look at this!" he exclaimed. "It all *starts* with my former colleagues in finance. They set the sales targets—to meet the short-term profitability goals of the company, of course. Sales managers adjust the CRM data to *prove* these targets can be met, and sales reps report overly-optimistic closing dates to keep management off their backs."

He was on a roll. "And, speaking of inaccurate reporting and wasting time, look at this." He presented a spreadsheet. "How much sales activity do you think happens each Friday at our call center? *Nothing at all!* They call it 'Siebel Day'—that's the CRM we use. Six months ago, the managing board noticed that the data in the system was so useless they demanded it be updated at the end of every week. That now takes a solid day from 34 people. We lose a month-and-a-half FTE[7] of selling time *every week* to update data that is obsolete by the following Tuesday!"

He paused while shaking his head in wonder. "And no one *sees* the system itself. No one understands how it's happening. That means no one can spot where it's failing. We can't really measure performance or figure out where people need to be developed. No wonder we're not hitting our targets!"

He turned to the subject of personnel management. "Hell, we can't even hire people right. We spend huge amounts of money to get rid of non-performers, and we'd already spent a huge amount of money hiring them because they supposedly *knew how to sell.*

"And we waste money on sales training by trying one thing after another that doesn't stick. It's no wonder my boss just told me he would only grant additional funds for training if I could guarantee that only high-performing salespeople would take it. And *that's* nuts. How do they become high-performing without the training?"

We talked a little more about the dysfunctional environment in which people were working—how it sustained itself even though it was producing sub-par results. We turned the conversation to the specific behavior of his salespeople in the field. *How* were they selling? What were they actually *doing* when they were with clients?

He shuffled through his notes to a section labeled "Behavior with Clients." This guy was good.

---

7   "Full-time equivalent"—one full-time salesperson

"Well, to begin with, the sales reps are friendly. They know which end of the fork to hold. They show up well, and they love to talk. In fact, they talk way too much. They actually talk *while* they're listening," he said with a grin. We asked him to elaborate, and he described how his sales reps *appeared* to be asking questions when they were actually steering the conversation in a certain direction.

He finished with a succinct observation. "All we do is *pitch*. That's what Jennifer spent four hours getting ready to do, and that's what she did for the entire hour we spent with the client. And most of the time, it just doesn't go anywhere."

"Any final conclusions about your selling system?" we asked.

He was quiet for a full three minutes. That's a long time in a busy restaurant. Finally, he summarized his findings.

"My people work in a high-stress environment," he said. "Their technical training is OK, but there's no visible selling system that everyone follows, no common language, and no clear developmental path. The company's processes drive them to waste a lot of time that would be better spent with clients. Although, when they're with clients, they talk too much and listen too little. When the clients resist in any way, they turn up the volume and keep pressing.

"This goes on for months, sometimes for years. Sales cycles stretch, and closing dates slip. Our managers work to keep the reps going, and the reps keep the deals going until the clients finally say, 'OK,' or refuse to keep talking. *That's* how we sell.

"As an analyst," he concluded, "I can tell you that it's a *lot* of input for a pretty meager output. And as a human being, I see that it's taking a huge toll on our salespeople, our managers, and our clients. In fact, I've done a few calculations…"

He pulled the last spreadsheet from his folder. On it were figures detailing the amount of money his division's inefficiencies and dysfunctional practices were costing the company. He had included the actual costs of firing low performers and hiring new people, and the opportunity cost of misspent time, low morale, and lack of selling skill. The bottom line was significant.

"This is what we're losing every day we continue as we are. This is my business case for changing the way we sell. Now, let's figure out how to fix this situation."

Pretty smart for a man who didn't know anything about sales.

IT AIN'T WHAT YOU DON'T KNOW

*"It ain't what you don't know that gets you into trouble.
It's what you're absolutely sure of that just ain't so."*
—ANONYMOUS, BUT OFTEN ATTRIBUTED TO MARK TWAIN

Colin had cracked open what he had described as the *black box* of how his division sold their products and what their inefficiencies, dysfunctional systems, and poor selling practices were costing the company. People behaved as if they knew exactly what they were doing. There were the perennial complaints about unfair compensation, uncooperative clients, and meetings that went nowhere, but nobody was calling into question the selling system itself. In fact, no one was even *asking* the question, "How *do* we actually sell around here?"

Colin's background in financial analysis gave him a keen eye, and his *lack* of sales experience gave him an open mind. That's a powerful combination. His investigation revealed what the science of transformative learning refers to as the *paradigm* in which his people were working—the set of processes and practices that his people were locked into and to which they kept defaulting.

> No one was even *asking* the question, "How *do* we actually sell around here?"

Paradigms are surprisingly resistant to change. From *inside* the paradigm, everything makes sense—it feels like you *have to* do things a certain way, even if they don't work particularly well. Furthermore, you just can't *talk* people out of their paradigm. One writer said that getting people to understand the paradigm in which they're stuck is like trying to get them to bite their own faces.[vi] Another described it as talking about freedom to prisoners who have forgotten that there's a life outside the prison walls.

Transformational science identifies ways to shift established paradigms. First, you have to help people see what they are losing, the price they are paying for continuing to operate as they are. Then you must help them uncover the *assumptions and convictions* that underlie how they've been behaving. You shine a light on the things that "everyone knows for sure that just ain't so" and see who wakes up to what's been happening. Then, if they *experience* behaving in a new way—if they can see and hear the benefit of doing so—things can actually change.

Colin was eager to take on this transformational work. He had nothing to defend and everything to contribute. He had taken the first step: recognizing that people were effectively *prisoners* of the selling system in which they were operating.

And he had discovered the fundamental *conviction* that was driving the system: that *selling is persuading people to buy stuff.*

The Prison[vii]

Picture a prison in which the inmates have been incarcerated for so long, they have completely forgotten that they used to have a life of freedom outside the prison walls. They no longer spend their time remembering how life used to be or planning for life following the completion of their sentences. Instead, all of their energy and activity is devoted to "getting ahead" within the prison. They compete for upgrades to their cells, awards for being productive prisoners, and recognition for contributions to prison art and literature—all of which support the notion that life in prison is all that exists.

There are therapists to help prisoners adjust to life behind bars, spiritual leaders to help them aspire to be the best prisoners they can be, and elected prison leaders who maintain the social order.

If anyone ever wonders, "Is this all there is?" they are quickly reassured that the answer to that question is, *"Yes, this is it."*

This common belief drives sales reps to prepare value propositions before they *or* their clients actually understand what's really needed. This belief drives salespeople to prove their value by *demonstrating* their expertise and *pitching* their products and services early in the sales conversation. This belief prizes talking over listening, persuading over inquiring, and convincing over educating.

And this conviction has a corresponding impact on clients. It drives them to be cautious about being persuaded and careful about revealing ignorance or weakness. They fear the silver-tongued salesperson who's out to manipulate their company into buying something they might not really need or want. It pushes companies to develop procurement processes that limit critical conversation between sellers and decision-makers.

And, ironically, it drives clients to *expect* sellers to pitch first and ask questions later. They actually *request* that salespeople show up and present their proposals, case studies, and proofs of concept. What if they did something different, like require sales reps to leave all that material at the office and, instead, use their expertise to help identify problems *before* offering solutions?

> He had discovered the fundamental *conviction* that was driving the system: that *selling is persuading people to buy stuff.*

Furthermore, this conviction—that selling is persuading people to buy stuff—has a detrimental effect on the entire sales team. Most sellers don't actually *enjoy* what it takes to constantly pitch, pursue, and persuade other human beings to sign a contract. It's not a lot of fun, and those sellers who *do* enjoy it turn out to be people you don't want to invite to the next family barbeque.

Lastly, sales *managers* have to somehow convince their salespeople to *keep* behaving like this: to keep pitching, pursuing, and persuading their clients to buy. How do they do this? By doing their own pitching, pursuing, and persuading—using both carrots and sticks to keep their salespeople's noses to the grindstone.

Colin saw all of this clearly, and he decided to buck the system. "Most of the sales execs around here care less about what and how the sales reps are doing than they do about the numbers coming in on time. I'll quit before I turn into that sort of manager."

With that declaration, Colin was ready to do whatever it took to create a *new* paradigm for selling within his division. He wanted a life *outside the prison walls*—for himself and for his people.

Executive Summary

You can't change what you can't see. Step one in any transformational process is to **perceive reality accurately**—to observe what people are actually saying and doing. That clear-eyed understanding of what's happening leads you to connect the dots in new ways—to see the **system** at work, the **prison** in which you're living. What are your salespeople actually doing with customers? What are your sales managers actually doing with your sellers? See this clearly, and, like Colin, you'll see the changes you want to make.

CHAPTER 4

DECISION INTELLIGENCE SELLING

Picture yourself in a training room—clean, comfortable chairs, coffee, tea, and juice at the ready.

Welcome to the first morning of your training. You've already met the trainer on a video conference, reviewing the performance profile you completed online.[8] It provided some helpful and reassuring insight about your own style of working. And it's got you wondering what your sales team—and your own manager—discovered about the way *they* sell and manage most effectively.

You look around the room. Your entire sales team is here, along with your boss. Surprisingly, your boss's boss is also present, along with the HR director and two senior sales specialists. These are people who know what they're doing, the people who lead change. It looks like the company means business.

---

8   We use the MRA profiling tool: see www.mra-ent.com.

At nine o'clock sharp, everyone introduces themselves, and you're underway. The trainer instructs you to find a colleague you don't normally spend time with and open your workbooks to page three. This question is written at the top of the page: "What do you *really* want from this training?"

You're given a few minutes of silence to reflect and write. Your first few sentences are the normal stuff—you want your team to hit their sales targets, quit complaining, and stop wasting time.

Then, you think more deeply. What you *really* want is for them to stop wasting *your* time: asking the same question in meeting after meeting, making you chase them for information they promised to provide, and expecting you to inspire and motivate them to do what they're being paid to do. The more you write, the more irritated you feel.

You want them to...*take charge.* Quit waiting for you to push them, direct them. And their attitude is inconsistent. You write, *I want them to be more positive.* You look at the word *positive*, and it doesn't really express what you're after. You want them to stop giving excuses and blaming external factors for what isn't working. You want them to just *get on with the job*, which is...talking to clients! Yes, it's about the *clients*.

> Your team spends too many hours *getting ready* to talk to clients.

Your team spends way too many hours *getting ready* to talk to clients. You remember years back to when you were selling. If you wanted to know what clients wanted or needed, you got off your butt, went to their offices, and, over a cup of coffee, you *asked* them. Many of your people seem to do anything but that.

Then you write the word *proactive. That's* what you want. Moving deals along *during* the quarter, not just at the end when the pressure is on. If anything, you want them to slow down at the end of a reporting period. All that rushed activity often results in shaky sales—poorly diagnosed, insufficiently designed, destined to cause problems downstream.

The trainer then asks you to share your thinking with a colleague. As you exchange thoughts with the person sitting next to you, you're surprised at the emotion you feel. You didn't realize how much this has been bothering you. You're actually relieved to be here with your team addressing these things. And you're beginning to wonder what *they* are writing about you and your management of them.

THE WAY IT'S BEEN

After the discussion, the trainer pulls the group together and invites everyone to start from scratch and forget everything they know about selling. He calls it "adopting a beginner's mind."

You turn to the next page in your workbook, where there is a pyramid-shaped diagram (see Figure 4.1). You start exploring the most basic style of selling. Passive selling is what you experience online or at retail outlets. At the grocery store, for example, there's never a salesperson who asks what you need and helps you find it. The sellers persuade you to buy certain items by shelving them at eye level. The more expensive products require you to "*raise your vision*" and find them on the top shelf. And the store brands, the white-label cheapos? You have to kneel down for those.

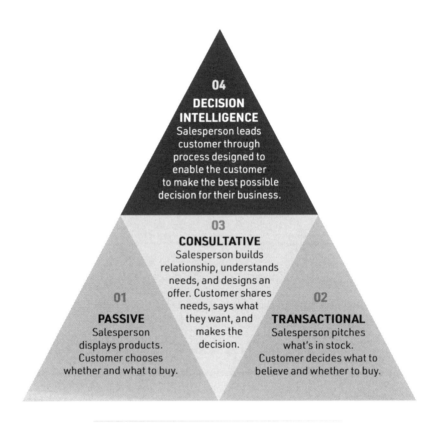

Figure 4.1 Four Ways to Sell

You roam the aisles alone, load your own basket, and, if you use the self-checkout register, the seller won't have to speak to you at all. A lot of science goes into this type of selling, and the results are invisible. The selling activity happens before you arrive.

The next type of selling can be called Transactional. This is what we normally think of as "selling." There's a conversation between the buyer and the seller. Sometimes, the buyer knows what they're after—a computer, software, equipment—and the seller has specific products to offer. At other times, the seller just shows up on the buyer's doorstep—or on the other end of the phone line—and is offering something they think the buyer might want.

The seller's job is to explain as quickly as possible the features, benefits, and advantages of the products they have on hand and then convince you to buy them. The customer's job is to sort out the wheat from the chaff, the reliable info from the pitch, and decide whether to buy or not. At best, the seller's pitch matches the client's needs. At worst, it can become an experience of forcing a square peg (what the seller has) into a round hole (what the buyer wants).

You're drawn to the next level in the pyramid, the one called Consultative selling. You've heard it called *strategic* selling and *solution* selling, and it is the sort of work your people do. Your products are most often sold B2B, and you have a wide range of accounts.

You are surprised to learn that this type of selling was officially labeled in the 1970s.[viii] The differences between transactional selling and consultative selling are interesting. You are reminded that the word *consultative* is derived from *consultant*, because the seller acts less like a *salesperson*—talking, demonstrating, and pitching—and more like a consultant—asking questions, listening, assuming the client knows what they need, and following the client's lead.

You flip your workbook back a couple of pages and add a sentence to what you want from the training: "Even when we think we're being consultative, we're actually just waiting for the moment to strike!"

You share this sentiment with the group. It draws a knowing, boisterous laughter. The trainer waits until everyone calms down and then asks, "So, what's so funny?"

The salespeople go quiet, waiting for you and the other three sales managers to speak first. You start to explain that you don't want to be inaccurate or unkind, and then you catch yourself. You were about to slip and slide like you normally do. *Screw it*, you think. *We're paying good money for this training, and I'm just going to lay it out there. If it creates a problem, well, that's what we're paying the trainers to handle.* You decide to go for it.

"My team knows that I sat in on a dozen client visits over the past three weeks. To be perfectly honest, I don't think any of you listened particularly deeply or well. It seems like you wait just long enough to hear the customer mention a need for a product we've got, and then you stop listening and start pitching. Do you think I'm wrong?"

> "You wait just long enough to hear the customer mention a need for a product we've got, and then you stop listening and start pitching."

This starts a 45-minute conversation in which you and your team share more truth than you have in months. It takes a while, but they finally admit you're right—they don't listen as well as they need to. But they are brutally honest about the amount of pressure they feel—yes, from you, but also from all levels of management and other departments—to close sales as quickly as possible.

There is one exchange that burns itself into your brain. It's with Mary, one of your senior salespeople and someone whose opinion you respect.

"Do you remember," she says, "that before the client meeting we took together last week, you said to me, 'Mary, we've *got* to get a buying decision *today*.' We didn't even have their needs defined yet, but you were pressing me hard to close."

You remind Mary that you were only reinforcing the closing date *she* had entered in the CRM. Mary takes a deep breath, glances around the room, and says, "Well, do *you* remember that I originally wanted that clos-

> "You told me I had to move the close date up so the sale would land in the previous month."

ing date to be four weeks later, but you told me I had to move it up so the sale would land in the previous month?" The room is completely silent.

Well, you think, *that* took guts. And yes, you do remember the conversation. Your manager had told you to make the CRM match the sales targets, and you'd done as you were told. You start thinking about the amount of pressure throughout the entire system and its impact on your sales force. The entire system is set up to press all of us to convince the client to buy as soon as possible.

You admit that Mary's recollection is accurate, and you acknowledge her for her honesty. That eases the tension in the room, and you can sense that it paves the way for more truth to be told. You're glad that over the years you've learned the value of humility.

The trainer turns the discussion to the *limitations* of consultative selling. They are easy to spot in your own organization. You see the overemphasis on *relationship building*—something that takes a lot of money, a lot of time, and, ironically, often *inhibits* the sharing of unpleasant but vital facts. You see the delays caused by salespeople who become hesitant to push clients forward. And you see how unrealistic it is to expect clients to self-diagnose the root causes of the problems that are in their way.

The trainer senses that this is a hot topic, and he gives everyone additional time to identify the breakdowns in your selling system. The group comes up with a long list. You're intrigued by the fact that many of the items are things you could fix yourself without having to get approval from higher-ups. That's promising.

Then, you realize that something even more interesting has happened. Somehow, during the past couple of hours, it's become apparent to everyone that the purpose and objective driving all three types of selling—passive, transactional, and consultative—is *persuading the client to buy.* It is so obvious that it's amazing no one has mentioned it before. It's like the Emperor's New Clothes—everyone sees the emperor is naked, but no one says so.

You have an insight. It's not that this purpose—*convincing clients to buy*—isn't right. It's that it just isn't right *enough.* Being *persuaded* isn't something most of your clients want to be put through. And it's not something most of your sales reps want to do.

When the conversation turns to the type of selling at the top of the pyramid, your ears are wide open.

THE WAY IT CAN BE

The trainer introduces a new line of inquiry. "Here's something that may strike you as strange, even impossible. But imagine what it would be like if your ultimate purpose in dealing with your clients was not to persuade them to buy, but to *increase their ability to make their very best buying decisions*—even if it meant they *didn't* buy from you."

You can feel resistance to this notion—in yourself and around the room. But you did commit to bringing an open mind, and you join a small group to consider it. The trainer adds some final instructions.

"Don't *debate* whether raising your client's ability to make the best buying decision is a better purpose than convincing them to buy. Just concentrate on what it would *be like* for you to sell this way. Be specific. How would you prepare for your first client visit? How would you behave during all your sales conversations? What would you say? What would you not say? How much would you talk? How much would you listen? And *when* would you talk, and when would you listen?

"Also, discuss what it would be like *for your clients* to be approached this way. What would be *their* experience if you weren't pitching and persuading? Go to work, see what you come up with."

> What would your client experience if you weren't pitching and persuading?

The discussion is eye-opening. What interests you most is how relaxed, enthusiastic, and engaged your salespeople are. The second thing you notice is how often they spot a process, a procedure, a standing meeting, or a policy that would have to change. And you realize that, yes, things will need to change, but it's exactly the sort of change your sellers and your clients would welcome. You're intrigued by this possibility.

Over lunch, there's a lot of conversation about what has to be different. Initially, you're concerned that some of the talk might just be the same old whine, but it doesn't turn out that way. Ben, for example, was talking again about the complexity of the compensation plan. You've heard him go on about this before, but this time he spoke with a different tone.

"I understand that figuring out how to pay us can be tricky—especially when we make a huge sale. Management doesn't know if we were keeping the deal in our back pocket when we projected our sales. Certainly, we've all done that before, just to keep them from raising our targets. But I've got some ideas about how all this could work better." That's the first time you've heard Ben talk solutions instead of just complaining about problems.

As the next session starts, you're expecting the trainer to begin with a new subject. Instead, he asks about the lunchtime discussion. Initially, you're impatient, but as you listen to your colleagues relate their thinking, you're intrigued. They are taking this seriously, and they're being seriously thoughtful. It's refreshing.

Now the trainer stands and turns to a flip chart. He draws the X- and Y-axes of a graph—only the Y-axis points down instead of up, and the numbers 0 and 10 appear at either end of the lines (see Figure 4.2).

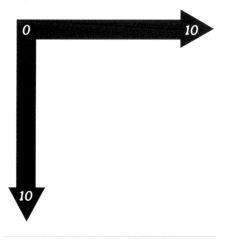

Figure 4.2 Decision Intelligence Selling

Problem

"As experienced salespeople," the trainer says, "you know that there are two fundamental things a client must fully understand if they are to have the information they need to make the most intelligent buying decision. What are they?"

Sarah raises her hand. "They've got to fully understand what we're offering." The trainer lets the answer hang in the air.

Ernesto breaks the silence. "But first, they've got to really understand what they need." Still no word from the trainer. His silence demands a deeper level of thinking. You notice the technique, and you make a note in your workbook to use it from now on in your one-to-ones with your direct reports.

In the discussion that follows, two of the senior salespeople criticize the practice of presenting solutions too early in the selling process. When the group finds its way to an agreement about this, the trainer labels the two lines on the graph. "OK," he says. "It's problem first and solution second." There is no disagreement.

"Furthermore," the trainer continues as he expands the diagram, "if clients have a rich and full understanding of all the problems they are trying to solve—a ten on a scale of one to ten—*and* they have an informed and comprehensive understanding of your proposed solution to solve those problems—again, an understanding to the maximum level of ten—would it be accurate to say they have 100% of the information they need to make their best buying decision (see Figure 4.3)?" Again, no disagreement.

> Raising a client's DQ *is* the focus and ultimate purpose of effective selling.

"This percentage is a measure of what we call Decision Intelligence or DQ," the trainer adds. "We're suggesting, of course, that raising a client's DQ *is* the focus and ultimate purpose of effective selling—*not* just getting them to buy. But that's simple to say and challenging to do."

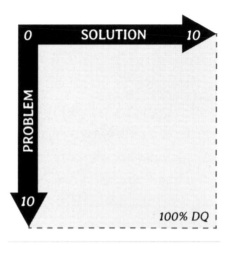

Figure 4.3 Decision Intelligence Selling

This stimulates a few minutes of discussion from the group. DQ is a novel idea. It's logical. It's a strangely attractive concept, something that sellers could actually *want* to do. But, like others in the group, you have questions about *how* to sell in this way. You wonder if upper management would even *let* you sell in this way.

"Well," the trainer says, "let's look at *how* to do this—starting with what it takes to lead clients to a deeper understanding of the problems they are trying to solve. This involves guiding them through two specific discussions.

"The first involves understanding and prioritizing *all* of the problems they have to solve. The second involves calculating the cost of leaving those problems unsolved (see Figure 4.4)."

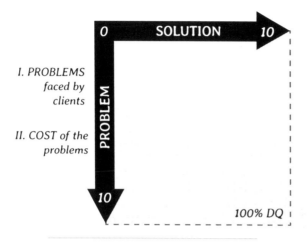

Figure 4.4 Decision Intelligence Selling

He writes the steps on the chart and says, "Let's talk first about getting the client—actually, *requiring* the client—to understand all of the challenges that stand between them and what they want. What's in *your* way of helping them do this?" The group has a lot to say.

"We can't take that much time."

"They come up with problems we can't solve."

"They don't actually know what's in the way—usually, we're talking to people who don't have sight of all the issues."

Susan, a new sales rep, chimes in. "And, what if they just don't *want* to tell us? That happens to me all the time. I know I need to ask about their challenges, but often they don't want to talk about them. They keep saying things like, 'You're the expert, tell us what we need…'" Here, she pauses, and several people complete her sentence.

"…and how much it's going to cost!" Everyone laughs.

"Those are some of the challenges," the trainer says. "And

you're going to get really good at handling them. But can we delay talking about this for a moment? I promise we'll come back to it."

The trainer asks for input on how sellers know a client has completed this first step. The discussion makes it obvious that what's needed is a written, prioritized list of problems to be solved. The group is thoughtful and vocal about the benefits of this list—for themselves *and* for their clients.

As sellers, this step gives them a more precise understanding of client needs. Furthermore, when their clients complete this list, it's an early buying signal and serves as a qualifying step in the process. Clients who don't have a clear picture of their problems find it very difficult to be satisfied with *any* solution.

> Clients who don't have a clear picture of their problems find it very difficult to be satisfied with *any* solution.

They also see that their clients gain a lot. Identifying and prioritizing their challenges usually requires the involvement of other stakeholders in the business. This creates greater buy-in and develops a clear agreement on the problems to be solved. And, most important of all, their clients develop trust—in the selling process itself and in them as sales reps.

Cost

The conversation then moves to the subject of getting the client to calculate how expensive it is to leave these problems unsolved.

"Would it be fair to say," the trainer begins, "that a client almost never figures out what their problems are costing them?

Let me tell you about a client we have really enjoyed working with—Greg Friedman, co-founder and CEO of Private Ocean Wealth Management in California."[9]

The trainer explains that, during the sales process, he and Greg had successfully completed a prioritized list of the problems he needed to solve to empower his financial advisors to raise assets under management (AUM) by 35% over the following year. Greg then asked how much it would cost to fix these problems and mentioned that he had a budget figure in mind.

You can see your sales reps leaning in. This is a familiar situation for them, and you know they don't handle it particularly well.

The trainer continues his story. "I asked Greg where he got his budget number. Greg smiled and said, 'I made it up.'" This draws a laugh from the group. At this point, they're liking Greg and maybe wishing their clients were more like him.

"He admitted that he didn't really know exactly what the budget should be to address these issues," said the trainer. "I suggested an exercise that would give him the information he needed to figure out exactly what he should spend and what he shouldn't. I told him the next step would be to calculate what it would *cost* him to *not* undertake any sales training, but just head into the next year doing the best they could with what they had. That would give him a solid figure on which to build a business case."

This is a stunningly simple idea, and your head fills with possibilities. It doesn't surprise you to hear the trainer say that

9   Greg Friedman has given permission to share his real name and that of his company.

Greg readily embraced the exercise. The trainer explains how he and Greg discussed ways to calculate the money he was *losing* by having these issues—money he was spending because the problems existed and money he was not earning because the problems were preventing his advisors from increasing their AUM.

The trainer says, "So, we each left that discussion with a task. Greg was to *conservatively* calculate the bottom-line cost to his firm of leaving his problems unsolved and then multiply that figure by the number of years he would suffer that loss. I was to draft a training program I thought would successfully solve the problems. We agreed to meet the following week."

Then the story gets *really* interesting.

"Our next meeting was a video conference. Greg brought his COO. The two of them were sitting at the end of a large table, across from one another. I could see both of them clearly, and that turned out to be a good thing. When I asked if he had completed his cost calculation, his COO picked up a piece of paper and said, 'Yes, I've got it right here,' and she took a breath, ready to share the calculation.

"I happened to notice that Greg clenched his hand, tensing his body as he straightened up in his chair. I reacted instinctively and said I didn't need to know the number, but *he* did. The fee for our services would be based on the time required for the project. He could use his cost figure to see if it was worth it or not to have us train his advisors. All *I* needed to know at the moment was whether or not the cost was high enough to have me present the training program I had drafted for the discussion.

"Greg smiled and said, 'You bet it is!' So, I started walking the two of them through the plan. We were five minutes into the discussion when Greg interrupted me.

"'Wait a minute. I've just got to tell you something.' He leaned back in his chair, shook his head, and laughed. 'You're not going to believe this, but last week I was sitting where you're sitting,' he said. 'My business partner and I were trying to get a competitor to sell us his company. We were digging, trying to get him to tell us how valuable the deal would be for him. Only, we were doing it to *figure out how much to offer them* for the company. When you told me you didn't need to know the cost number, that's when I knew you could be trusted. You weren't manipulating me; you were simply helping me to get the information *I* needed to make a good business decision.'"

The trainer talks a little longer about how this was a turning point in the client relationship. The cost discussion had called forth honesty and integrity from both parties. Impressive.

The Cost discussion had called forth honesty and integrity from both parties.

Again, you separate into small groups, this time with different colleagues. Your task is to make a thorough calculation of the cost some of your clients—existing and prior—were actually paying for leaving their problems unsolved. Your group discusses three clients, utilizing hindsight to calculate the cost of the problems they really did have. When you return to the large group, the combined insight of the shares is extraordinary. The cost list is long and detailed. And when calculated over multiple years, the total is huge.

The trainer captures this information on multiple flip chart pages, hangs them around the room, and then asks a simple question: "What are the benefits of requiring your client to make this calculation?"

The group offers several answers. It gives clients a huge wake-up call about the money they are losing. It demonstrates the price of delay and slowdown in their buying process. It creates a foundation for a business case to buy your product. It generates trust in your selling process and differentiates you in the marketplace because few other sellers do this. Perhaps most important, it gives a hard figure that *replaces* the budget amount a client may have brought to the discussion. Now they have a real, critical financial figure to compare with your eventual proposal.

Things are making sense. The sales specialist adds a final thought: that calculating the cost is a *qualifier*—if the cost isn't high enough, the client's not going to buy anyway. It's better to find this out before investing the time to develop a solution and prepare a proposal.

You're beginning to see how this can work. As you look around the room, you can see that you're not alone.

Solution

After a coffee break, the trainer turns to the Solution axis of the graph. "Just as there are two steps required for your client to fully grasp their problems, there are two steps to comprehending your solution." The trainer writes "Solution" and "Value" on the diagram (see Figure 4.5).

Now, you're on familiar ground. Your team knows how to develop proposals—how to illustrate them, and how to present them. They've been doing this for years, except they've been doing it too early in the process. The advantage of waiting until this point to develop a solution is clear. Now you know what's important to include and what can be left out or postponed.

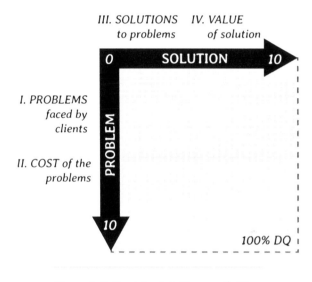

Figure 4.5 Decision Intelligence Selling

The trainer talks more about the solution step. To make the process collaborative, it's important to get the right people in the room—the client's people and your own people. And, when presenting the draft solution, it's important to *not* include pricing. *That's* a new thought. And an intriguing one.

It takes the room half an hour to discuss and digest the options here. It's not that there's one right way to do it, it's that this approach—getting collaborative agreement on the solution *before* pricing it—creates the focus and clarity that effective solutions require. And you will certainly save your own company money, time, and all the problems associated with selling something that would have been difficult to deliver. The service department is going to love you for this.

Value

"OK," the trainer says, "the client now understands your draft solution. They've collaborated with you on its development and agreed to a course of action. There is still one more step to take before you write a proposal that includes the price you're going to charge. It's critical that your client becomes fully aware of what this solution will do for their business. That's the step we call Estimating the Value of the Solution."

You sense where the trainer is heading, and the light goes on about the importance of having this financial calculation. These figures—both cost and value—give clients an objective way to evaluate your price. They are a critical part of the business case that the entire DQ selling process has helped them build. Now they are ready to greet your final proposal with an informed and open mind.

The group discussion is lively and thorough. They have numerous examples of helping clients identify where solutions will save money or generate revenue. What's new for them is realizing the impact of *collaborating* with clients in this process—it creates ownership of the solution and confidence that it will pay off.

Mary has an additional insight. "You've already got the client's agreement about everything that needs to be in the proposal. That alone is a great pre-close step. And if the client has concerns about the price tag, we don't just have to resort to a discount. We can make the case that lowering the price limits the extent of the solution, which means that not all their problems will be solved, and not all the value will be realized. This is a great way to manage the client's expectations."

You sense that the discussion has landed on solid ground. Raising the customer's DQ has brought reality into the room. Of course you can't reduce the price without compromising the quality of the solution. Your mind starts to imagine a scenario of you actually saying this to a client when the trainer interrupts your thoughts.

> Raising the customer's DQ brought reality into the room.

"How many of you suspect that your clients aren't coming to that first meeting with you expecting to take these four steps?" Most of the group raise their hands, and several of them share their experience of clients *beginning* the sales conversation with requests for information, case studies, proposals, proofs of concept, and, of course, pricing information.

"Let me show you why they do that," the trainer offers. He points at the Problem axis. "Think about your most savvy clients. On a scale of one to ten, how deep does their understanding go about all the problems they are trying to solve *and* the price they're paying by leaving them unsolved?"

The group reflects on the initial selling conversations they've had with clients in the past. How aware *were* their clients of the full extent of Problem and Cost? They come up with an average rating of 8 for their most sophisticated clients and 3 for their least savvy clients. Then, they score their clients on the solution axis. Their most experienced clients score a 6—they don't know anything yet about the solutions your business may be offering—and the least sophisticated clients score a 3.

The trainer draws some dotted lines on the graph, creating three squares as he plots their responses (see Figure 4.6). Even the smartest clients only have a 48% DQ. The least informed clients have a staggeringly low 9% DQ. Now it makes sense why clients often begin with questions about your company, your products and services, and how much they cost. They're covering up the gap in their DQ, even if they're not aware of doing so!

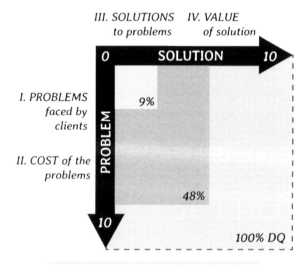

Figure 4.6 Decision Intelligence Selling

The trainer adds four words to the diagram on the flip chart and presents the *experience* a client has during this four-step journey (see Figure 4.7). As customers deepen their awareness of their challenges, they feel more concerned. When they calculate the cost, they feel a sense of urgency. The understanding that there is a solution to meet these challenges brings relief and confidence that they're on the right track. And estimating the value of that solution generates a willingness to invest.

I. Problems	→	CONCERN
II. Cost	→	URGENCY
III. Solutions	→	CONFIDENCE
IV. Value	→	WILLINGNESS

Figure 4.7 Impact of DQ Selling on Clients

You make a note in your workbook: *Our people have a lot to learn about walking clients through these four steps!*

"Does it always work? Do clients always agree to go through each step?" the trainer asks. "Of course not, but that's the point. The four stages also serve as a *qualification* process. If clients don't want to complete the steps, the red flags should start waving. We've learned the hard way that skipping steps doesn't make the issues disappear—it just delays them until you're ready to close the deal. Then they show up as objections."

Now that the stages are understood, the group starts asking a *lot* of questions about *how* to lead clients through the process. And now that they are seeing the possibility of transforming the way they sell, it's time to tackle the second transformation: *building* everyone's ability—the sales reps, the managers, and the specialists—to *lead* clients through this process and *develop* a selling system that keeps everyone on track and continuing to master these skills.

> "I could get up in the morning and do *this* for the rest of my life."

It's like a switch flips in your brain. You've just made a decision. This is the way you want your people to sell from now on. You don't know how you're going to do it, but you know you're going to make it happen. This could change *everything*.

And Mary's final comment nails it for you. "I don't know about the rest of you, but I could get up in the morning and do *this* for the rest of my life."

Executive Summary

Our clients have applied the principles of Decision Intelligence Selling to a variety of sales situations: B2B and B2C, transactional and complex, hard products and soft services. Once you step beyond the old paradigm of sales being an activity involving pitching, pursuing, and persuading, you can create a selling approach that is dedicated to raising the DQ of your clients. This requires leading them through a four-stage process, focusing successively on Problem, Cost, Solution, and Value, *before* presenting a final proposal for your goods and services. This creates trust and loyalty in your clients, and it requires your salespeople to be worthy of that loyalty and trust. This changes everything.

PART THREE

TRANSFORMING THE PEOPLE WHO SELL

CHAPTER 5

ASLEEP AT THE WHEEL

If you're serious about transforming the way your salespeople perform, there is a fundamental question you must address first: *why is it so difficult for people to change the way they think and act?*

When it comes to changing the way we think about sales and how we do it, this is a profound problem to understand and to solve. We've taught thousands of salespeople to *raise the DQ of their clients* instead *of pitching and persuading* them. They greatly prefer selling like this, and they are very surprised by how difficult it is to change their ways.

Transformative science points out that every one of us used to be *great* at changing ourselves. We all had five uninterrupted years of *daily* transformation. If you want to watch this happening, spend time with a young child. Unless children are subjected to extreme conditions, their first five years are filled with one incredible change after another. They *naturally and easily* learn to move, to speak—several languages, if they're in the right environment—to sing, draw, dance, write, count, think for themselves, and know what they want.

What changed between those early years and where we are now? What happened that made us so resistant to changing the way we operate? How did we walk into prison with our eyes wide open, thinking it looked like home?

> What happened that made us so resistant to changing the way we operate?

THE AUTOPILOT PARADOX

Modern neuroscience describes the development of what philosophers and theologians have long called the *human condition*. Around the age of five, our brains develop a self-reflective ability that starts *making up our minds* for us. It draws conclusions about everything that happens to us, tells us how to respond, and predicts what will happen if we don't follow its directions.[ix]

If this is the first time you've heard about this mental development, it may seem too fantastic to be true. But spend some time listening to your own thinking, and you'll discover just how accurate it is.

All of us who have had small children can remember moments when, seemingly overnight, they became convinced that they could no longer do something that, up to that moment, they'd been doing naturally and with great enjoyment. "I can't draw" or "I can't play piano" or "I'm no good at math" are the things parents start hearing from their six and seven-year-olds. Where did those conclusions come from? From the same place your salespeople are listening to when they say, "Closing is just hard for me," or "I always get nervous when clients object."

Research estimates your brain produces 2,000-3,000 thoughts per hour, each requiring 1/25 of a second to influence your thinking and your behavior.[x] This barrage of unnoticed input has been building ever since you were about five years old. By the time you were twenty, it had formed your personality and locked you into patterns of thought and action that *felt natural,* like you'd *always* been that way.

> Around the age of five, our brains develop a self-reflective ability that starts *making up our minds* for us.

This conditioning process—which automates our behavior—actually has a positive purpose, which is probably why our brains evolved in this way. As fast as your mind works, it is still way too slow to respond to situations that call for an instant reaction—like a bus bearing down on you. There's a neurological circuit that bypasses this self-reflective part of your brain and goes straight to a motor center that causes you to jump to safety.

Even in non-threatening situations, the operating circuitry of your brain—think RAM storage on a computer—just isn't big enough to consciously consider everything you do each day. For example, when you were learning to drive, do you remember how hard it was to think about everything that had to be done? Both hands on the wheel. Press the accelerator, but not too hard. Keep an eye on the rearview mirror and the side mirrors. Remember to signal for a turn, figure out when to start the turn, and when to release the wheel to make the car go straight again. And parking—OMG, parallel parking! Now, years later, you get in your car, speed along, navigate heavy traffic, and arrive safely at your destination—all without ever actually thinking about what you're doing.

This is the upside of *living on autopilot.* It's a necessity for getting through the day. If you had to *think* about everything you did—walking, talking, opening doors—you'd get very little done. The brain, however, doesn't content itself with automating everyday tasks. It's an automating machine, and it tries to automate *everything*—including, for example, the way you think, feel, and react to clients and colleagues who look a certain way or say certain things. Autopilot is very effective for certain everyday tasks, but it's extremely unhelpful when it comes to sales and sales management.

Take a close look at your own sales teams. How many of these well-intentioned and highly-skilled people react to surprises and challenges the same way they've been reacting for years? You can sit in your office and *predict* what they're going to do.

How much of your management time is devoted to trying to change the *circumstances* they are dealing with because you can't figure out how to help them change their *reaction* to these circumstances? When salespeople and sales managers live on autopilot, they grow accustomed to—they feel comfortable with, they settle for—doing and saying things that limit their professional performance and reduce their personal fulfillment.

Autopilot is easy to spot once you know what you're looking for.

Fortunately, autopilot is easy to spot once you know what you're looking for. Apply Einstein's definition of insanity, and notice where your salespeople are "doing the same thing over and over again, expecting a different result." Keep a sharp eye out for what's called 'polarity' behavior. This is when salespeople or sales managers shift from one ineffective behavior to its opposite. They stick with something until it's overwhelmingly obvious it isn't working. They have a strong emotional reaction to failing, and then they do something quite different. When that doesn't work, they flip back to what they did before. Here are two real-life examples.

A SALESPERSON ON AUTOPILOT

Edward was an experienced salesperson, having worked for his current company, SpecializedTech, for twelve years. Over time, he had worked his way up the ladder until he was in charge of several key accounts, including a lucrative trading company called New World Investments (NWI).

Edward's contact at NWI was an experienced procurement officer named Solaire. When Edward first met Solaire, he was cautioned by his sales manager that some repair work was needed. Edward's predecessor had grown increasingly frustrated with Solaire's style and pace of communication, and his angry confrontation with her resulted in a call from NWI's CEO requesting that the account manager be replaced.

Relating

Edward made it a priority to re-build the relationship and restart the deal. He developed long lists of questions, he listened deeply, and he prepared numerous iterations of sales proposals. He remained patient when Solaire skipped meetings, missed deadlines, and failed to provide information.

"I've got this," he told his manager. "It's taking a lot of time, but it's buying goodwill, and she seems pleased." He genuinely liked Solaire, felt empathy for her circumstances, and enjoyed his time with her. His manager kept complimenting him on his communication, both to NWI and internally to his own company. It all looked good.

Feeling Frustrated and Conned

At the three-month point, Edward noticed the deal wasn't really progressing. Solaire still hadn't given him access to the technical people and key decision-makers at NWI. She kept asking for more reports, more case studies, more quotes. She repeatedly told him, "Things are moving along nicely," but he had a sinking feeling that they weren't.

"I think I'm getting strung along," Edward told a colleague over drinks one evening. The next morning, when his manager said, "Maybe you're just too nice of a guy to close this deal," Edward's frustration turned into humiliation.

> She repeatedly told him, "Things are moving along nicely," but he had a sinking feeling that they weren't.

Enough was enough. It was time to *make* things happen.

Asserting

Over the next few weeks, he became far more direct with Solaire. Following every conversation, he sent an email clearly spelling out what Solaire had agreed to do and by when. When she missed a deadline, he immediately pointed it out, often with less tact than he had previously employed. He pressed harder to meet the other key people at NWI, he challenged her thinking, and he refused to accept her excuses at face value.

"Now, I'm getting somewhere," he told his manager at the weekly team meeting. "I'm not taking any more sh*t, and there are no more free lunches until she delivers the goods." He was proud of himself. Clearly, his gentle approach to building the relationship with Solaire hadn't been working. But he had made the required adjustment. Now, *she* was the one playing nice— apologizing for delays, complaining about the internal politics that stood in her way and asking him to understand.

"I don't really enjoy being like this," he said to his wife one evening, "but it seems that this is what it takes to succeed. I've got her backed into a corner, and it will be over soon." He noticed that his wife didn't say anything.

He continued working this way for a few more weeks. Then, things blew up.

Feeling Exhausted and Embarrassed

Late on a Friday afternoon, Edward's manager called him into his office. "I know you've been working hard on the NWI account, and I've been letting you do it your way. I took you at your word that you were getting somewhere, but Solaire's manager—a friend of mine—just phoned to warn me that Solaire is beginning to complain that you're being a jerk. You've obviously pissed her off somehow, and you might be putting this deal at risk. I'm giving you the weekend to think about what you're going to do differently."

Edward went straight home. He was out of gas. He had knocked himself out to challenge and correct the evasive and contradictory messages from his client. He was tired of chasing

Solaire around the block, and he was tired of his manager's scrutiny and pressure.

When he told his wife what had happened, including how he'd changed his approach, she said something surprising: "You sound embarrassed." *That* was a revelation. All the tough guy stuff, the take-no-prisoners behavior, the pressure tactics to move his client along—this just wasn't *him*. He'd done what he thought he *had* to do, but he didn't *want* to do it anymore. And he certainly didn't want to do it for the rest of his career at SpecializedTech.

That evening, he decided that he had to do what *felt right*—he had to *reconnect* with his client, keep things *positive*, and *trust* her to do the right thing. It had been a mistake to lean on her, and he needed to reestablish the good feeling that had fueled their relationship in the beginning. He would stop putting on the pressure, schedule a workshop to clear the air, and get things back on track.

He set out the next morning to rebuild his relationship with Solaire. He was confident that he was on the right path. He didn't even suspect that what felt like progress was actually traveling in a circle (see Figure 5.1)

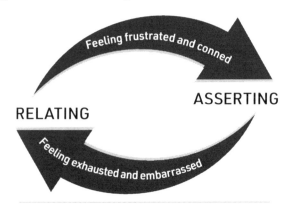

Figure 5.1 Salesperson on Autopilot

A SALES MANAGER ON AUTOPILOT

When we sat down with Faith for the first time, she was discouraged and ready to quit. She was the sales director *and* the sales manager for a business in New Zealand called Solar For People. She directed the work of a small but growing sales force offering solar installation for other small- and medium-sized enterprises.

"When I was hired a year ago, our CEO was very direct about what she expected. None of my predecessors had been able to get our sales team to raise the average number of products sold each month from its pitiful level of 2.3. I've been here a year," she said. "I had a fast start, and sales jumped. Then, something stopped working. Now, we're back to where we started."

We asked her to walk us through her work over the previous twelve months—what had she done, the results she had accomplished, and the changes she'd made along the way.

Directing

"When I arrived," she said, "the sales force was a mess. There was no discipline, little motivation, and massive confusion. These people needed direction, and they needed it now. I took the sales target the CEO gave me and divided it equally among the team members—no special treatment. I promised them a hefty commission if they succeeded and dismissal if they didn't. I knew it was harsh. I told them I was tough but fair. I would put in the time to manage each of them, and, in turn, I expected them to follow my direction, work hard, and reap the rewards."

During the next three months, Faith kept her word. She spent hours with each salesperson. She traveled with them to the field, coached them as they worked, directed their movement, sorted out territory disputes, established deadlines, and controlled every step of the sales operation.

"The Q1 results were brilliant!" she said. "Our average number of sales per person jumped to 3.8. It was worth all the effort."

Feeling Exhausted and Trapped

Then, in the second quarter, sales fell by 20%. She was concerned, but she didn't panic. She kept up the pace until, two months into Q3, the wheels started to come off. Several people got ill or said they were. And she noticed a big jump in the number of complaints she was hearing from her direct reports. They complained about colleagues who got in their way, about installers who failed to show on time or did shoddy work, about finance managers who kept asking them to handle collections on loan payments, and about company executives who made surprise visits and kept criticizing the pace and size of sales.

The complaints had one thing in common: somehow, it was Faith's fault that things weren't working out. It seemed like everyone agreed that she was too demanding, too autocratic, too bossy, and too pushy. They had gone along with her autocratic leadership style, but that was obviously failing. If only she would give them more room, trust them more, they would do a better job.

"That just pissed me off," she said. "I was knocking myself out for them, and all they could do was whine." She paused, sat back in her chair, and took a breath. "I took it personally. Two of my top salespeople left—that really hurt—and, by the end of the quarter, sales were off by an additional 65%."

She took another breath and continued.

"When the HR manager started questioning my management style, I really started doubting myself: *What if they're right? What if I am being too hard on people? There's just one of me. I can't be everywhere.* I had to do something different."

At that point, the HR manager formally intervened. He sat Faith down for a heart-to-heart conversation. After two hours, Faith concluded that being directive just wasn't working—it didn't actually change people for the better. She *had* been micromanaging, trying to control her people instead of letting go of the reins. A different approach was required. She needed to demonstrate trust and confidence in her people in order to stop their criticism and bring out their best. She needed to give them a chance to show what they could do and set them free to fly.

Trusting

She spent several more hours with the HR director, developing a comprehensive plan for a "more enlightened" style of sales management. When she was ready, she called a four-hour team meeting to lay out her new strategy to salvage the final quarter of the year.

"It was exciting, actually. I told them that I had heard their complaints, that I knew I had been too controlling, and that things were going to change. I let them know that they mattered to me on a personal level and that I was going to trust them from now on to perform at their best. I asked each person to write a statement of intention—a manifesto declaring the commitment and purpose they would bring to their work. I asked them to develop their own targets and activity plan, and I spent the next week meeting individually with each of them to review their thinking."

Her sales team reacted with a mixture of curiosity and disbelief. The older reps were cynical, and the newer people were confused. They were relieved when Faith approved their self-chosen sales targets. They didn't know that the total of their targets was 17% less than their previous quotas, leaving Faith with zero margin to work with for her own performance. Everyone had to hit their targets, or she would fail to hit hers. "I figured I'd better trust the process," she said. "I didn't want to pour cold water on their enthusiasm. They actually were happier than I'd seen them in ages."

The next month did indeed show improvement. The number of sales calls was up, a few small business deals closed that had been hanging out for weeks, and most of her team seemed more energetic than they had been. HR was off her back, and she was feeling pretty good about what she was doing.

That only lasted for sixty days. Now, as we were talking to her, she could see that this particular strategy was doomed.

Feeling Frustrated and Out of Control

"We are closing in on year-end," she continued. "The team is all relaxed and happy, but sales are crap. We're going to finish Q4 dead even with where we started Q1. Nobody's going to hit their self-chosen target, I'm certainly not going to make my number, and *none of them seem particularly bothered* by this utter and complete failure."

"Everyone cheered. That's when I knew I'd screwed up."

She paused a moment as if deciding whether or not to say what she was thinking. She took a breath and continued. "Last

Friday, we were at the bar for our weekly happy hour. Several of them were on their third round and feeling no pain. Jorge raised his glass in my direction and shouted, 'To the best boss in the world. I *love* not having to report my stats every week!' Everyone cheered. That's when I knew I'd screwed up."

Faith had thought that taking the pressure off people would appeal to their sense of responsibility and result in them tracking their own data, taking charge of their professional development, and hitting—even exceeding—their sales targets. Instead, while letting go of

"Why repeat what didn't work in the first place?"

control had bought a lot of goodwill, it had actually led to a decline in performance. She threw her hands in the air and said, "I don't know what to do! I'm back where I started. My manager is leaning on me to get things under control, but that's what I did a year ago. Why repeat what didn't work in the first place?" At least Faith was *noticing* the loop she was stuck in, even if she didn't know what to do about it (see Figure 5.2).

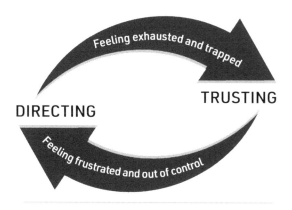

Figure 5.2 Sales Manager on Autopilot

We expect that, somewhere in these two stories, you can see yourself and your teams. Edward's automatic cycle is an example of how sales reps often bounce back and forth from *relating to their clients* to *persuading them*. Faith's cycle similarly describes the two behaviors that sales managers often adopt: being *directive* or being *trusting*. The point here is that *all* of these behaviors—and flipping back and forth between them—are examples of automaticity. When one strategy backfires, people on autopilot don't have the breathing room to try something really new. Instead, they revert to what they know. They default to habit.

And that takes us to an insight from transformational science that our clients have found extremely helpful as they lead the change process in their companies.

NEVER TRUST A HABIT

We've spent this chapter looking at the very human problem of falling into unconscious, automatic behavior. As one of our early transformational trainers said to us, "It's not your fault that you 'go automatic,' but it *is* your responsibility to do something about it."

With that in mind, consider this definition of a habit:

> *A settled disposition or tendency to act in a certain way, especially one acquired by frequent repetition of the same act until it becomes almost or quite involuntary.*[xi]

And here is a neuroscientist commenting on how the brain works:

> *Brains are in the business of gathering information and steering behavior appropriately. It doesn't matter whether consciousness is involved in the decision making. And most of the time, it's not.*[xii]

And last but not least, some traditional wisdom putting it metaphorically and bluntly:

> *Man is asleep. Must he die before he wakes?*[xiii]

When it comes to selling, it's obvious that effective habits are better than ineffective ones. There are truckloads of books on personal and professional development aimed at helping people establish healthy, productive behaviors. But transformational science raises a caution flag about seeking to develop *habits*.

> The fundamental problem with habitual behavior is that it's *unconscious, not chosen.*

The fundamental problem with habitual behavior is that it's *unconscious, not chosen.* Once you stop choosing what you do, you lose the ability to choose something *different.* You lose what you were born with—the ability to change when you want to. Regaining that *natural ability* to transform yourself is the key to high performance—not just in sales, but in life.

And the first step in regaining that ability is to *notice* when you've fallen into autopilot, *refuse* to lurch to previous habits, and *choose* your next step based on what really matters to you.

That's why our clients focus on developing the right *practices* instead of better habits. You *choose* practices; they *don't* become automatic. And if you *find yourself* doing a practice out of habit, it's a good idea to stop, take a breath, locate your purpose for what you're about to do, and then *choose* the practice or *choose* to do something else.

This focus on *making choices,* moment-by-moment, is what wakes us up from living on autopilot. It brings clearer thinking, confident decisions, and wiser actions. You access what you lost early in life: freedom, flexibility, and boldness.

Gaining this access is actually a very simple process. It involves learning how to bring what's called "present-moment awareness" to whatever you're doing. This is a skill that can be learned, and, when you practice it, a natural, inherent *brilliance* emerges. It sounds a bit magical—and it actually *feels* a bit magical when it happens—but in fact, it's a natural process that neuroscience refers to as *developing new neural pathways.* We call it Rewiring, and it happens as you rise to the challenge of transforming yourself and the way you sell.

That's what this part of the book is all about: how to put transformational science to work for you and your sales force. You don't have to be concerned about the number of ineffective habits your people already have or how long they've had them. Get the right practices in place—the practices that *require* people to become *awake and aware,* to turn off their autopilot and make a free choice—and the *activity of selling becomes a transformational force* within your entire company. Structure your sales process around this possibility, and some very interesting things start happening.

Now, let's look at four fundamental practices you can use to transform the way you and your people sell.

Executive Summary

There's a fundamental, very human problem standing in the way of transforming the people who do your selling. It's the way their brains developed early in childhood. Around the age of five, our minds start to *automate* the way we think and act. *Living on autopilot* slowly replaces the ability to think outside-the-box, to notice when you're running in circles instead of moving forward and when you're operating on habit instead of real, free choice.

To turn off the autopilot takes both awareness and skill. We've been looking at the need to wake up and notice whatever selling behaviors you're caught in, the good habits as well as the bad ones. Now we turn to four *practices* that create the conditions in which you and your people can transform the way you sell—the way you think about it and the way you actually do it.

CHAPTER 6

AIM YOUR BRAIN

"Would you tell me, please, which way I ought to go from here?"
"That depends a good deal on where you want to get to,"
said the Cat. "I don't much care where—" said Alice.
"Then it doesn't matter which way you go," said the Cat.
—LEWIS CARROLL, *ALICE'S ADVENTURES IN WONDERLAND*[XIV]

Sales transformation is about transforming *results*. Any activity that doesn't ultimately result in greater sales performance is not an activity worthy of your time and money.

We like the saying, "At the end of the quarter, you will either have the sales results you're after, or you'll have all the reasons you couldn't get them." Results or reasons—it's direct, it's stark, and it's a dose of reality. The problem is

> Results or reasons—it's direct, it's stark, and it's a dose of reality.

that, while it's true, it doesn't focus people on what they need to *do* to get the sales results they're after.

From a transformational perspective, the *first* thing a sales force needs to do is to *aim* themselves at the *right* things. This chapter is about how to do this consistently and well.

AIMING YOUR BRAIN

The Cheshire Cat was right. If you don't know your destination, it doesn't much matter which way you go. The situation is slightly more complicated for your sales force. The destination is probably well-identified; they have sales targets, right? What's probably not so clear is the *path* to hit those targets—what to do and when to do it to avoid wasting your time and squandering your resources.

There is a lot written about self-management skills—how to manage information flow, develop priorities, handle to-do lists, email, and the like. A lot of it is good, even brilliant.[xv] A transformational perspective, however, focuses on a more fundamental challenge that must be dealt with *first* if these skills are to be used effectively.

> Your brain drives you in many different directions, and you don't always know that it's doing it!

This deeper challenge is noticing and accepting two critical things that happen often each day: your brain drives you in many different directions, and you don't always know that it's doing it! As one of our early mentors once asked, "Who's aiming your brain, and what are you going to do about it?"

The first book we read about this was initially published in 1960.[xvi] It asserted that the human brain, weighing about three pounds and containing billions of neurons and trillions of synapses, is built to *fulfill commands*, to be *aimed* at some goal or objective.

This is easy to demonstrate. Take a moment and imagine a purple elephant with pink polka dots. Did you notice that you could *see* this elephant in your imagination? Your brain created that mental image in response to the instruction.

This process happens automatically. And, as we've already mentioned, it's how our minds mislead us, starting around the age of five: interpreting what happens, telling us what to do, and generating anxiety and fear about the future. You can watch this happen right now: just put down this book and set a timer for five minutes. Close your eyes and pay attention to your own thoughts as they fire off, wander around, and pull you this way and that.

This is the autopilot at work. And quietly, underneath your conscious awareness, *this* is what's aiming your brain! This is how we lose the power of choice and fall into autopilot without knowing it's happening.

This automatic aiming goes on morning, noon, and night. It pulls your salespeople and sales managers off track by providing *other* targets for them to pursue—other things that, for the moment, seem important and valuable, but which ultimately interfere with fulfilling their sales objectives.

You may have a sales rep who believes he's committed to a particular sales result, but he's actually *more* committed to avoiding criticism, looking good, finding an excuse, or a dozen other things—all of which pull his focus and energy away from what he needs to do to sell effectively.

He can learn how to aim his brain instead of letting it aim itself.

You and he are very aware of the fact he's missing his target, but what's harder to see is all of the *automatic aims* that take his eye off his target— things that draw him away from his intended path, keep him from thinking clearly, tempt him into wasting time, make him nervous when his clients object, and render him clumsy when it comes time to close.

But he actually can learn a time-tested way to regain control of this process—how to aim his brain instead of letting it aim itself. It starts with learning how to access what is called his Deep Desire.

Competing for Your Attention

An esoteric teacher was talking to a friend who was arguing that human beings had free will.[xvii] "Ah," said the teacher. "I'll show you free will." He drew a circle with many squares inside it, each of which contained a capital I.

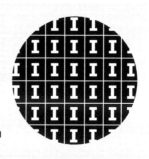

"A person wakes up in the morning, and one of his I's says, 'I want to go to work.' Immediately, another I speaks up, and says, 'I want to stay in bed.' Two minutes later, another one pipes up, 'I'm hungry.' Another says, 'I'm too fat. I need to skip breakfast.' It goes on like that all day long. *That's* what people call free will."

UNLEASHING DEEP DESIRE

The word *unleashing* is dramatic. We chose it because discovering what you *really* want often brings an explosion of inventiveness, originality, and boldness. It *feels* dramatic.

We're thinking of Charles, a senior vice president who managed the global sales activity of the highest revenue-producing division in his company. He was on the third day of his face-to-face training with his senior sales team. It had been enlightening for his sales managers to explore the *many I's* that interfered with leading their sales teams—the many *aims* that distracted them from what they needed to do. They were intrigued by the concept of Deep Desire as a way to increase their ability to focus and direct themselves. Charles is a lead-from-the-front kind of guy, so he volunteered to demonstrate the process.

He took a moment to quiet his thinking and place his full attention on his quarterly sales target. Then, he started to talk about what he *wanted*.

"I want to support my team to lead their teams to produce 640 million dollars top-line revenue."

"And you want that," said the trainer, "because you want...what?"

Charles thought a moment, and then said, "I want to hit my target...no, I want to *smash* my target."

"And you want that because you want...?"

"I want a big bonus!" Lots of laughter and some applause from his team.

"And you want a big bonus because you want...?" Charles picked up the pattern and continued on his own. He talked about his three children and the schools he wanted to send them to. He shared his desire to fund a family vacation in Greece. And he mentioned a long-standing dream of a country home that he and his wife had been wanting.

Then, he went deeper. After some silence, he said quietly, "And I want my team to have whatever *they* want for their families." He carried on without waiting to be prompted by the trainer. "And more than that, I want them to be happy in their work… fulfilled…enjoying this job we all spend 70 hours a week at."

This continued for a few more minutes. Charles talked about his desire to not be just a good boss, but a great one. He wanted his direct reports to look back on his time with them and regard him as one of the best managers they'd ever had.

Finally, he ran out of words, out of wants. At the trainer's last prompt—"And, you want that because…"—he said, "It's just the way I am."

The trainer was smart enough to stay silent. The room felt somehow bigger. This experience was different than creating one more plan to achieve a goal. Charles had accessed his Deep Desire. He knew it. The group knew it. The brightness in his eyes confirmed it.

The trainer asked one last question. "Now, as you sit here, feeling what you're feeling, what is your very next step—the very next thing you're going to do to move toward those things you most deeply want?"

Charles stayed silent for another minute before adding, "I'm going to finish this training with my team, and we're going to put it into practice. We're going to change things for good around here."

Take a few minutes and try this for yourself. Pick a goal that matters to you. Create some room to be quiet and focused. Pick up pen and paper and start digging for why you *really* want to achieve that goal. A simple statement starts the process: "I want…" Take that statement deeper by completing the sentence with, "And I want that because I want…" You can alter the words as you go: "I want that because my intention is to…," "…my purpose is to…," "what I want to create is…" Just keep digging, breathing, feeling—see where it takes you.

This is a simple but profound exercise.[xviii] Practice it regularly and you will find your unique reasons for doing things large and small, and you will generate the motivation to see them through. You will transform your pursuit of sales results by solidifying your resolve, inspiring your creativity, and sharpening your focus. You'll be in control of where you're going and what you're doing to get there.

If you're going to do this, however, be aware that you won't be as easy to work with as you were before.

> **Aiming opens the door to peak performance.**

You'll push back more on people, policies, and procedures that block your movement forward. No matter what arises, you'll always find a way to stay on course.

This is the power of *aiming*. The discovery of your deepest desires—and using them to achieve your professional goals—gives you the ability to turn off your autopilot. You spend more time aiming your brain, and your brain spends less time aiming you.

It's a remarkable transition. Sometimes, you notice the results right away. At other times, a few weeks pass before you realize your anxiety has gone down, your confidence has risen, and your actions are decisive and effective. Aiming opens the door to peak performance.

EYES ON THE PRIZE

Once you learn how to actually *aim* your brain, the question for sales professionals becomes, "What do I aim *at?*"

This is the task Mark Jopling and his team tackled on the second day of their training.[10] They were searching for the *inputs* that would deliver the *outputs*—the specific selling activities that would deliver the sales results they all wanted.

"What must our clients *do* at each of these four points to fully develop their decision intelligence?"

"Obviously," said Patricia, one of Mark's managers, "we've got to figure out how to *support* our clients to make better decisions for themselves." This was interesting. The team was settling into the new paradigm for their selling activity: they were focusing their attention on what *clients* would need to do in order to fully understand Problem, Cost, Solution, and Value. Patricia formed the question that led them forward: "What must our clients *do* at each of these four points to fully develop their decision intelligence?"

Figuring this out took more time than they expected—mapping the process from the *client's* perspective was harder than it looked, but the result was worth the effort. When they were done, they had identified the specific stages their clients had to pass through in order to develop a high level of decision intelligence.

---

10   We introduced Mark Jopling in Chapter 1.

Each stage was a step in the journey, a step that clients had to take if they were to understand the problems they were trying to solve, grasp the solutions that would solve them, and build a solid business case.

When Mark's team looked at what they had created—a ten-stage journey their *clients* had to take—their next task was obvious. They mapped the actions their *sales reps* needed to take to *lead* their clients through these stages. They posted their work on the training room wall (see Figure 6.1).

The group stayed quiet for a few minutes; then, individual managers offered their observations.

"This is going to work," the first one said. "We were good before, but if we follow this process, we're going to shoot the lights out!"

> **"*This* is how our sales reps become trusted advisors."**

"If, and I mean *if*," his colleague replied, "we can get our teams to be disciplined about this, we'll know exactly where we are at every point in the sale."

"And that means we can intervene when we need to..." said another.

"And stay the hell out of their lives when we don't!" said Mark.

They kept building their understanding of what was possible. It was clear that the purpose of their new *selling* process was to facilitate the client's *buying* process. The higher the client's DQ, the better the client's buying decision. The better the buying decision, the greater the client's trust in the solution and the salesperson. All of this would undoubtedly increase overall customer satisfaction and increase the chances of repeat business and referrals.

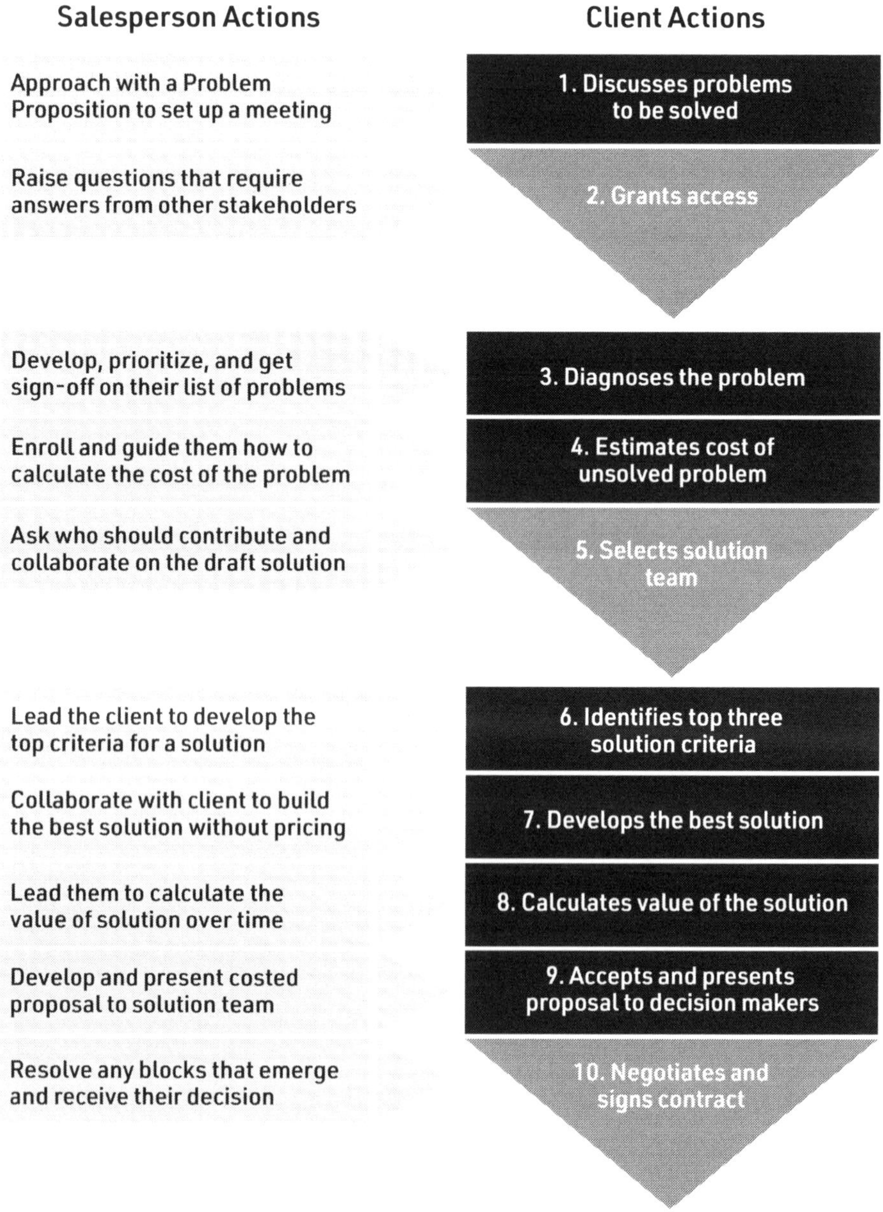

Salesperson Actions	Client Actions
Approach with a Problem Proposition to set up a meeting	1. Discusses problems to be solved
Raise questions that require answers from other stakeholders	2. Grants access
Develop, prioritize, and get sign-off on their list of problems	3. Diagnoses the problem
Enroll and guide them how to calculate the cost of the problem	4. Estimates cost of unsolved problem
Ask who should contribute and collaborate on the draft solution	5. Selects solution team
Lead the client to develop the top criteria for a solution	6. Identifies top three solution criteria
Collaborate with client to build the best solution without pricing	7. Develops the best solution
Lead them to calculate the value of solution over time	8. Calculates value of the solution
Develop and present costed proposal to solution team	9. Accepts and presents proposal to decision makers
Resolve any blocks that emerge and receive their decision	10. Negotiates and signs contract

Figure 6.1 Leading Clients to Develop Their DQ

"*Nobody* is selling like this," Mark's longest-serving manager said. "This is how we're going to differentiate ourselves from our competitors." He thought a moment and then added, "*This is how our sales reps become trusted advisors.*" "And now we've got a system that *we* can trust," another manager added. "Now, we *know* what it takes to move a deal through the pipeline with precision and certainty—including when to let a deal go. We can track whether or not our reps and our clients are taking the right steps at the right time."

"And," said another member of the team, a data specialist, "if we can track it, we can train it—we can measure how effective each rep is at every step in the process. Then we'll know exactly how to keep everyone improving."

Two weeks later, Mark shared with us that this moment was a turning point in the training. When his direct reports figured out their selling system and did it together, his group of highly talented, individualistic, and competitive senior leaders became a *team—and that's when he knew it would* work.

Your system—the steps *your* clients need to take to develop their DQ and the things your salespeople need to do to *lead* their clients through these steps—will be unique to your business. Just follow the DQ stages, in order—

> Just follow the DQ stages, in order— Problem, Cost, Solution, Value—and you'll figure it out.

Problem, Cost, Solution, Value—and you'll figure it out. Once these inputs are established, you've got a path for your salespeople to follow in order to create the results your company needs.

Now, let's take a look at how to create the conditions that will require and empower your salespeople and sales managers to engage your clients in this way.

We start with the most critical skill of the bunch: how your people can manage their attitude, their state of mind, moment-by-moment as they work. This is the fastest, surest, and most effective way for people to turn off their autopilot and engage their natural brilliance.

Executive Summary

To utilize the transformational formula—R=A+C+E—you need to discover the Results you *really* want to create. Start with your professional objectives, especially your sales targets. But don't stop there. Dig deeper for the *wants-under-the-wants*—what *really* matters to you.

This is how you take charge of *aiming your brain*. Either you control this process, or it will control you. And you know where *that* leads. Master the practice of aiming, and you'll be amazed by how your brain starts working for you instead of against you.

To know what to aim *at*, identify the stages of the journey your clients must take to develop their DQ—the decisions they must make and the actions they must take. Then, identify what your sales reps must do to *lead* your clients through these stages. Now you've got a process that your people can follow, step-by-step, client-by-client, to meet and even exceed their sales targets in a genuinely sustainable way.

CHAPTER 7

MASTER YOUR ATTITUDE

The purpose...is to help you find what you think you already have, namely free will, intelligence, and self-consciousness. I expect you to find this idea preposterous.
—DR. CHARLES T. TART[XIX]

Attitude is the "A" in the transformational formula, R=A+C+E (see Figure 2.1). Learning to manage it moment-by-moment is the fastest and surest way to raise the level of your salespeople's performance. For most sales leaders, however, that is easier said than done. As one of our clients, a senior sales VP, said: "Attitude is everything. I know when it's right, but I don't know what to do when it's wrong."

> "Attitude is everything. I know when it's right, but I don't know what to do when it's wrong."

This is where the insights and practices of transformative learning are invaluable. They demystify mindset—what causes it and what changes it. Master the ability to help people change their state of mind, and you become a leader that builds your people instead of merely organizing them and riding herd as they work.

The first step in becoming such a leader is to face an unpleasant, even brutal truth—a truth that does indeed sound *preposterous*: most of us spend a *staggering* amount of time on auto-pilot. People who haven't discovered their own automaticity find this hard to believe. But anyone who's attempted to change the way they work or the way their direct reports work knows how difficult it is to *notice* our ineffective behavior, *admit* it's not working, and *change* the way we work. When people are stuck in autopilot, those are exactly the three things they can't do. Instead, they *explain* why their actions should have worked, *blame* someone or something else for why they didn't, and *repeat* the behavior, hoping this time they will succeed.

> Most of us spend a *staggering* amount of time on autopilot.

In fact, we are so used to working on autopilot that it often takes a shock to the system to get our attention. We *do* receive these shocks—the surprises, disappointments, and failures that we didn't want or expect—we just don't know how to *use* them to wake up, turn off the autopilot, and choose to do something new. This ability to wake up is what we lost starting around age five. Fortunately, we can find it again.

We find it interesting that an increasing number of companies are experimenting with mindfulness training. It's taken nearly six decades for corporate leaders to "discover" the value of a quiet mind and a calm center. These are invaluable assets when it comes to navigating the challenges and pressures of the business world, especially the world of sales. But Eastern practices can be a difficult fit for the Western workplace.

The problem is that mindful awareness is usually taught in ways that borrow from its origins in the Buddhist tradition—this involves one form or another of meditation, sitting quietly for a period of time focusing your attention inward. This is a valuable practice, but it has significant limitations in the business world.

Often, the good feeling generated by thirty minutes of meditation fails to last through the first coffee break of the day. And when the pressure is on, and you-know-what is hitting the fan, you can't say to your client or your colleague, "Excuse me, I need to meditate for a while so that I can stand to be in the same room with you!"

> You can't say to your client or your colleague, "Excuse me, I need to meditate for a while so that I can stand to be in the same room with you!"

Two things are needed to successfully *integrate* mindful awareness into daily work so that *becoming* mindful doesn't require you to stop working. First, you've got to wake up—*become* aware that you're on automatic, that you've *gone back to sleep.* Then you need to know *how* to turn off the autopilot *without* withdrawing from whatever you're doing or whomever you're with. Both are skills that can be learned and used to bring your best to what you're doing.

The most effective way to notice when you've fallen into autopilot is to pay attention to your attitude, your state of mind. It's not difficult to do. You just have to know what to look for.

ABOVE-THE-LINE AND BELOW-THE-LINE

Recently, one of our trainers was teaching attitude management to a group of sales executives. She drew a horizontal line across the middle of a flip chart page (see Figure 7.1).

Figure 7.1 Above-the-Line and Below-the-Line

"We've all had periods of time—an hour, a few hours, maybe even an entire day—in which our attitude, our state of mind, was really *up*," she said. "When was the last time that happened for you? What was it like?"

The answers came slowly at first. Then they picked up speed. The trainer wrote them above the line as they tumbled out: *exciting, fun, creative, easy, productive, relaxed, focused,* and *strong.*

"And if those *up* times included challenges, difficulties, problems to solve?"

The group offered more description: "The problem didn't seem that big," "I was unstoppable," "I always had options."

The trainer's next question—"And how did you feel?"— evoked their emotions. The group talked about feeling powerful, strong, in control, bold, and confident. A sense of quiet strength entered the room, and the trainer let the silence linger.

Then she asked, "Now, what's your life like when you're feeling *down* instead of up?" A new set of words and phrases emerged, and the trainer wrote them below the horizontal line: *confused, uncertain, unfocused, angry, inflexible, I couldn't get it right, nothing worked,* and *I should have just gone home.*

The trainer kept collecting their descriptions of everyday experiences—feelings, thoughts, and behaviors—and writing them on the flip chart either above or below the line. She allowed enough time for their awareness to grow, and then she said, "Attitude really isn't more complicated than this. Every minute of every day, you're either *above* this line or *below* it." She asked them to discuss this in small groups for a few minutes. Then, she took them to the next level.

"There are actually *different* states of mind that we slip into during the day, depending on what happens to us. There's a spectrum of mindset, from very high to very low (see Figure 7.2)."[xx]

The group spent some time exploring the six different levels of attitude. They started by remembering moments when they were so *up* that nothing could get in their way. No matter the obstacle, the challenge, or the issue, they could always think of *other possibilities*—there was always a way over, under, around, or through whatever they were facing. Their creativity was a match for any problem, and their level of job satisfaction increased with the level of challenge. "When I am in that state of mind," the sales director said, "I'm fearless."

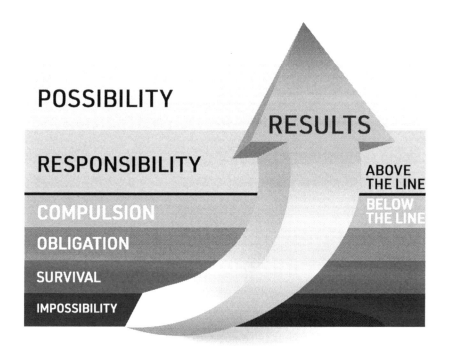

Figure 7.2 The Attitude Spectrum

"When I am in that state of mind," the sales director said, "I'm fearless."

The attitude just below Possibility— still above the line, just not as *high* a state of mind—resonated with the newest senior manager in the group. "I've just been given my first team to manage," she said. "My seven direct reports have very different personalities, and three of them are actually failing at their jobs.

I can honestly say that I don't know what to do...*yet.* What I *do* know is that I'll figure it out and make it work."

At that moment, she was the picture of Responsibility. She was committed, willing to learn, and fully accepting of the challenge in front of her. Nobody in the room doubted she would find her way forward, one way or another.

The attitude that was hardest for the group to identify was the first mindset below the line. "It's not a surprise that you're struggling with this," the trainer said. "Compulsion *feels* like Responsibility—strong, vigorous, active, in control. And, frankly, in many sales organizations, Compulsion passes for peak performance. Compared to the three states below it, it looks great, and you *do* get results. In this state of mind, salespeople work harder, keep pressing, and don't give up—no matter how they feel or what happens."

"They also burn out, blow up, and drive the rest of us crazy," one manager said. The group laughed in agreement and traded reminders of times when they or their colleagues had operated in this state of mind. They knew well its aggressiveness, perfectionism, and intolerance. And they also knew its impact on clients who strongly disliked being maneuvered.

The company's co-founder and CEO was eloquent. "I spent years in Compulsion. In fact, I built this company with that attitude." He paused a moment for emphasis. "And it cost me my marriage, a number of friendships, and nearly my life." Now, two heart attacks later and with a new spouse, he was encouraging his people not to follow his example.

The descent into the next three levels of mindset was easier to spot. The group shared several experiences of falling into

Obligation: describing it as *"running out of gas" after* a period of compulsive activity. "I spent the month with zero motivation," said one analyst. "I was always on time to work, but never early. And I always *left* on time. I did what was expected, but nothing extra."

This burst of all honesty opened the door for even more comments about the panic people felt when their mindset fell into Survival. "During the final quarter of last year, when my team was so far off target, I ran around like a headless chicken," said one manager. "And nearly everything I did just created more of a mess. We didn't hit our target, nobody got their bonus, two of my best people quit, and the rest of the team fell into Impossibility—they were working, but, really, they'd given up. And, I must admit, I gave up on them. I guess I was in Impossibility too. I've spent the last three months trying to recover. What a waste."

The trainer pointed at the diagram and asked a final question. "What does the upward arrow indicate?" In spite of the word "Results" written in the arrow, it was a surprisingly long time before the group finally realized the impact that their state of mind has on their *ability* to produce sales results.

This connection between attitude and results is one of the most fascinating contributions of transformational science to sales performance. The teacher we spoke of earlier, who diagramed a human being as a collection of I's, called this process the development of an *Observing I*—an active, conscious *awareness* of what the rest of our mental machinery is doing. Step one is to watch your state of mind as it slides up and down the Attitude Spectrum during the day. Step two is being patient with yourself—accepting your frustration and embarrassment about being Below-the-Line.

Once you *know* you're Below-the-Line, there's only one sensible thing to do: return to a more productive state of mind. To do this, we recommend a simple practice called Split Attention.

SPLIT ATTENTION

Split Attention[xxi] is a transformational practice that links early spiritual training to modern neuroscience, which has confirmed the brain's ability to develop new neural pathways—to *rewire* itself and make new behavior possible.[xxii] Its great advantage is that *you can do it while you're working* (see Figure 7.3).

> Its great advantage is that *you can do it while you're working*.

There's a video on our website that will guide you through the technique.[11] Sometimes, people can learn the technique by reading about it, so here is an explanation.

Keep the majority of your attention on whoever you're with or whatever you're doing. At the same time, *become aware of* something physical, something you can *feel*. You can pick *any* physical sensation. We have found two that work most often for the people we train: the movement of their stomachs while they breathe or touching two fingers to a thumb.

---

11 www.wrpartnership.com.

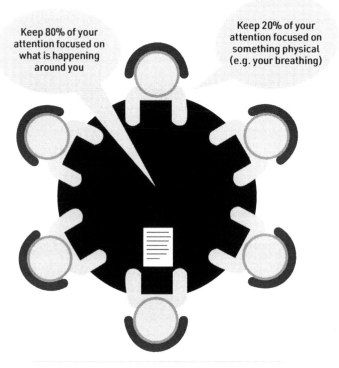

Figure 7.3 Split Attention

For example, if you're listening to a client or a colleague, *continue* to listen *while* you feel your stomach push out as you inhale and pull back in as you exhale. You can try it now while you're reading these words. Read this paragraph again slowly. As you read, *feel* your stomach expand and contract as you breathe. See if you can do this for an entire breath while you keep reading.

Try it again, re-reading the paragraph as you *feel* your first two fingers touching your thumb.

Go ahead. Read other paragraphs, alternating feeling your stomach movement with feeling the touch of your fingers.

Which sensation is easier to pay attention to as you read—your stomach moving with your breath or the touch of your fingers and thumb? You may find, as we do, that *breathing* is easier to focus on when you're listening, and *touching* is easier when you're speaking. Experiment. Find what works best for *you*.

You'll probably find that you can only stay aware of splitting your attention for 15 or 20 seconds at a time. You drift away from it until the next time you remember to split your attention. So, practicing this technique is a humbling experience. Don't try to *do it all the time;* instead, *return to it* as often as you can. When people practice split attention eight to ten times a day, they spend a lot more time Above-the-Line where greater results are possible.

It's so simple to do, and it's so hard to *remember* to do it. This fact, however, makes it ideal for professionals who work in teams. When somebody's attitude is *down,* he or she is often the last to know. Colleagues can help each other notice when Split Attention is needed.

Our clients often put *this* part of the training to work immediately. Within a couple of weeks, sales managers report that "Are you Above- or Below-the-Line?" has become a common and helpful question. And "Let's split our attention together and get back Above-the-Line" has become critical to clear thinking and wise action.

We have found that awareness of the Attitude Spectrum and using Split Attention are quite possibly the most important things we've ever learned about transforming human performance. Everything else follows.

GETTING HIGH(ER)

Once you start practicing Split Attention with some regularity, you can use it to *accelerate* a skill we've already shared: uncovering your *Deep Desire* and finding a purpose and motivation that can fuel your highest performance.[12]

It's easy to do. Split your attention for a few moments. Then, focus on something you want, and use the phrases "I want… and I want that because I want…"

Stick with it. Keep returning to splitting your attention while you write. You will find that it raises your attitude quickly, clarifies your thinking, and develops a resolve that takes you forward.

Not bad for an investment of three to five minutes.

When you get good at this, you can even do it mentally *while* you work. For example, let's say you're in the middle of a conversation that turns difficult. You notice yourself slip Below-the-Line. You ask the other person a question, and, while they're beginning to respond, you split your attention and mentally say to yourself, *What I want right now is…and I want that because what I'm after is this….* When you get good at this, you can elevate your attitude in seconds.

Like a ski instructor once told us, "This is a mileage sport." You learn it by doing it. It's OK to fail. Keep practicing. The payoff is huge.

Now, let's take a look at how to use Split Attention *and* have a conversation with *anybody*— clients, colleagues, managers, family, and friends—that has the best chance of drawing them

---

12   We introduced Deep Desire in Chapter 6.

Above-the-Line and having them join you in committing to actions that move things forward.

Executive Summary

Attitude is central to success. You can learn to manage it moment-by-moment as you work. When you do, you access a profound and naturally high-performing capacity within yourself. From ages zero to five, you lived in that state nearly full-time. You can use Split Attention to bring yourself into the present moment *as you work*. Combine it with discovering your Deep Desire, and you can spend a lot more of your professional hours Above-the-Line instead of Below-the-Line. The impact is immediate and compelling.

Split Attention is an inherent part of our transformational selling practices. In the next chapter, you will see how to use it while leading clients and colleagues in conversations that generate understanding, agreement, and committed action.

CHAPTER 8

GENERATE COMPELLING CONVERSATIONS

The sales training industry is saturated with technique—how to dress, how to mirror your client, how and when to ask the right questions, and, of course, how to close the sale.

A transformational approach to *Competence*—the "C" in R=A+C+E—is actually to *step away* from the "Three Ts:" tips, tricks, and techniques. Instead, transformative learning suggests that you focus on *context*—that is, a *way* to be with people that *creates the conditions* for two things to happen: everyone gets Above-the-Line, and everyone commits to actions that move things forward. These two things occur when salespeople listen more and talk less.

> Most salespeople *love* to talk.

Unfortunately, most salespeople *love* to talk. It's part of their gift. And the existing sales paradigm, which focuses on pitching and persuading, begs salespeople to open their mouths instead of their ears. Most sales managers know this is a problem. Over and over again, they watch their reps fail to listen long enough to learn the breadth and depth of the problems their clients face. Instead, when the first need appears, they jump into action and go for the sale. They miss opportunities for larger sales and wind up pursuing deals that are ultimately less helpful to the client. Reps don't listen long enough when they think their job is to pitch.

THE ITCH TO PITCH

Why do salespeople pitch more than they listen? Because *everyone expects it.*

Your *company* expects it. They require your reps to show up for client visits with a value proposition, a case study, a brochure, or a slide deck in order to describe what they're offering, prove that it works, and paint mental pictures for the client about what it will do for them. The meta-message in this preparation is not *Show up and listen*, but instead *Go forth and pitch.*

Your *clients* expect it. They're used to "being sold." They'll deflect your questions and *demand* that you pitch them: *Show me what you've got. Tell me about your company. Why should I buy from you instead of your competitors?*

Your *salespeople* expect it. They think their credibility and trustworthiness come from explaining what they're selling and demonstrating its superiority. They actually believe that the more eloquent and persuasive they are about the product or service, the greater their chances of making the sale.

But, what if everyone realized that demonstrating product knowledge and pitching clients *doesn't* really establish credibility and raise a client's trust? What if salespeople recognized that arriving with a pitch and a demo makes them *indistinguishable* from their competition? What if they grasped that *nobody* really finds this process helpful or enjoyable?

> What if everyone realized that demonstrating product knowledge and pitching clients *doesn't* really establish credibility and raise a client's trust?

So *how* does a sales rep do something different, something that actually *leads* clients to the discoveries that enable them to buy wisely and be confident in their decision?

And, how do sales managers do something different with their teams, something that genuinely empowers them instead of oscillating between micromanaging them or leaving them to their own devices?

Let's return to the training room to learn how to do this.

CREATING COMMITTED ACTION

Transformational training has its unique demands. It's not straightforward, and it doesn't "follow the manual." You have to lead people through a fresh, often surprising *experience*, get them to share that experience with their colleagues, and then recognize how they've changed. You can't do this by following specific steps. The best you can do is to keep splitting your attention, stay Above-the-Line, and trust that every human being longs to wake up and start thinking for themselves.

We join one of these trainers—we'll call him John—who's working with a group of sales professionals—three sales managers and their teams. It's the third day of training, and everyone is feeling at home. They've just finished discussing the challenges of facing clients who are suspicious, resistant to reveal that they don't know everything, and actively working to keep the sales rep from having direct contact with other people in the company.

John decides to go straight for it. "Is it OK with you if I ask you to do an exercise without explaining why we're doing it?" The group has zero resistance, and John asks everyone to choose a partner with whom they're willing to have a serious conversation.

The tension rises a bit, but people pair up. John introduces the exercise. "To make this real, instead of a role play about talking with a client about a deal, you're going to have a conversation with a colleague about a challenge they're currently facing at work. Once you learn the *framework* involved in this conversation, you'll be able to apply it when you're with your clients, your direct reports, your colleagues, and anyone else you speak with."

John asks for a volunteer, and Alexander joins him at the front of the room. John draws a vertical line on a flip chart page, dividing the page into two sections (see Figure 8.1). He says to the group, "Watch what I do." He turns to Alexander and asks him to describe his challenge.

"Well," Alexander begins, "I've already spoken to my manager about this, so I'm not talking out of school." He nods at Thomas, his manager, who nods back. "I'm running into a brick wall with one of my clients, and I don't know what to do. They've gone radio silent for six weeks now. I've sent several emails and phoned a few times, but nothing's happening."

Figure 8.1 Precision Listening

John writes a few words and a symbol in the left column of the flip chart page: "brick wall," "6 wks," "emails," "phone," "to do?" He circles "6 wks" and draws an arrow from it to the right-hand column, where he puts a question mark. He turns to Alexander and says, "So, you've hit a brick wall with your client, they're not responding, it's been six weeks, and you don't know what to do."

John doesn't say anything else. He looks at Alexander and waits for him to continue.

"Uh, do I just continue to talk?" Alexander asks. John just smiles, the group laughs nervously, and Alexander takes a breath. Then he carries on, his voice a little stronger. "I think

I've waited too long, actually. But I didn't want to push him. I did that once before and got into trouble. I didn't want to make the same mistake twice."

As Alexander spoke, John made a few more notes and then said, "You didn't want to repeat your earlier mistake, but you do think you've waited too long."

This time, Alexander didn't hesitate. "Yes, I tend to do that. Sometimes I'm just not bold enough. I don't know why. And it's crazy, actually. I've done a really good job building this relationship. He really does trust me, and I do see a way to find out what's going on."

John kept taking notes on both the left and right sides of the vertical line, pausing every minute or so to play back to Alexander what he had said. In response, Alexander thought more deeply, and within a few minutes, he had developed two possible strategies for reengaging with his client.

After ten minutes, John stopped the conversation and asked the group, "What did you see me do with Alexander?"

People noticed several things. John had faithfully repeated back to Alexander the main points of what he was saying, sometimes even using his exact words. One person noticed that John used his notes to remember what Alexander had said. Another noticed that John hadn't referred to any of his notes on the *right* side of the line.

John was itching to make some points, but he stayed disciplined about listening for *their* insights before sharing his own. "And," he asked, "what did I *not* do?"

Several people responded. "You didn't ask any questions." "You didn't offer any suggestions." "You didn't steer the conversation—you just stayed quiet...*I could never do that.*"

John kept the conversation on track. "We'll talk later about how to use this skill in real conversations—we call it Precision Listening, by the way. But here's an important question: what *happened* to Alexander when I *didn't* ask any questions, make any suggestions, or guide him in any particular direction?"

Alexander spoke first. "I solved my own problem!" *This* was a revelation. John wondered if the three sales managers were thinking more deeply about how to talk with their direct reports, and he made a mental note to bring it up later if they didn't mention it first.

**"You just stayed quiet...
I *could never* do that."**

After more discussion, John decided it was time for the group to stop talking and start practicing. He directed them to workbook pages that were blank except for the vertical line. "Make your notes about what your *colleague* says on the left side of the line," he said. "As you think of things you want to ask or say, put those notes on the *right* side of the line. Every couple of minutes, play back what *they* said, but keep your *own* thoughts and questions to yourself."

John coached each pair as they worked. He felt excited when someone listened well, and he managed his frustration when they didn't. He did a good job giving short, helpful directions to the person who was doing the listening.

As he moved from pair to pair, people appreciated his interventions, and he felt pleased with the quality of his coaching. Then, he encountered a crusty, senior salesman named Felipe who blurted out, "Why are we doing this?" John spent a full minute explaining the purpose of the exercise before he realized he was Below-the-Line. He split his attention, relaxed, and said,

"Felipe, I'm wasting your practice time. I know this seems strange, and you're not the only one with that question. I'll make you a deal. You just keep practicing, and I'll answer your question when we get the group back together. OK?" Felipe agreed, and John moved on to the next pair.

After a few more minutes, John gathered the group together. The shares were animated and revealing.

"I've never had anyone just listen while I talked. It gave me time to realize what I really thought," said one of the sales managers.

> "I've never had anyone just listen while I talked. It gave me time to realize what I really thought."

"My colleague really *did* know what to do," said another of the managers. "I'm so used to thinking I have to solve everybody's problem that I could hardly keep my mouth shut!" There were some knowing smiles around the room.

"I just had a revelation," said Edward, a newer sales rep. "The more that Sarah listened to me," he paused and nodded at the woman sitting next to him, "the more I relaxed. When she gave me room to talk at my own pace and didn't try to pull anything out of me, I actually shared more than I was planning to. It's strange, but the more she listened like that, the more I *trusted* her."

This last comment got the group thinking about the impact on their clients. What if they "lingered longer"—that was Edward's phrase—on whatever the client found interesting and valuable to say? Peter raised his hand and spoke slowly. "I think I'm getting something here. If I stop jumping on the *first* sales opportunity that appears, if I stop trying to steer the client to what I want to offer, I bet that a lot more opportunities will appear." The group talked a while longer, sharing their new insights about the power of listening deeply and well.

After a few more minutes, John was ready to introduce the next step. He noticed Felipe looking at him, and he remembered his promise. "Felipe raised a question that I'm guessing many of you have," he said. "How many of you thought you'd never behave like this in a real conversation?" Half the group raised their hands. Felipe looked triumphant. A few more questions revealed the issue for everyone. It was the *silence* that was difficult to handle—not adding anything after playing back what their partner said *and* staying quiet while their colleague pondered what to say next.

John said, "In sales conversations, it's helpful to leave a bit of silence—people need room to think—but you don't want to let the silence get long and awkward. It's too uncomfortable. Just be careful not to do things that *take the conversation away* from the client—like introducing another subject or asking a question that pulls them a new direction.

"Here's a simple way to handle the silence," John suggested. "Look at the left-hand side of your notes, find something they've *already said* that you're curious about. Then say, 'Tell me more about this.'"

This simple idea struck a chord not only with the sales reps but also with the managers. It was non-manipulative and non-controlling, and it provided a way to keep the other person moving forward, digging deeper, investing more in the conversation.

The discussion started to slow down, and just when John was wondering if it was time to move things forward, Helen put her hand up. "I've just realized something," she said. "By following my colleague's lead, I've learned things I wouldn't have thought to ask. And it's given me time to develop a few ideas about what he can do to handle the challenge he's facing. They might be helpful, and I do want to share them."

John smiled to himself at this reminder of the saying that "*everything works* in the training room"—the group will let you know when to move on. "Yes, that's the next step," he said. "Look at your notes on the right-hand side of the page. You'll probably find that some of those things are no longer necessary to mention. And some are *very* necessary. You may have questions. You may have guidance. You may think something they are planning to do is brilliant or a huge mistake.

"Say what you think. See what happens. *They* have the responsibility of deciding what to do. What they need from *you* is your honest and direct opinion before they make that decision."

The pairs launched into spirited conversation. John didn't coach them this time. He watched them work and felt the energy and vitality that filled the room.

When this part of the exercise was complete, he gave a final instruction. "You've listened deeply and without interruption as your colleagues explored their challenges. You've offered your own honest opinions about what they're facing. What's the obvious next step? What's going to make this conversation worth having invested your time, instead of becoming one more discussion that doesn't go anywhere?"

One of the junior salespeople nailed it. "Ask them what they're going to *do* about it!"

"Exactly," said John. "But here's a way to do it that will actually work. Don't ask them for a plan; ask for a very next step

(VNS)."[xxiii] A brief discussion follows in which many people acknowledge their paralyzing habit of developing elaborate plans before taking action. Identifying the *very* next thing to do to start resolving their challenge, and then doing it *before* deciding the next step, felt faster and freer. It only took a few minutes for each pair of colleagues to decide what they would do next and when they would do it.

John then added a final element to the process: "Ask your colleague if there's *anything* that could get in the way of taking their very next step." After a short discussion, five people had fine-tuned what they were going to do. This proved the point. It's easy to fall back into autopilot and overlook what's standing in your way. And it's easy to avoid this if someone asks you to take a closer look. Simple and helpful.

John introduced the conversational framework they had just experienced. "It's called CLEAR," he said, "and I use it to guide *every* conversation I have—whether I'm selling to a client, managing a direct report, working with a colleague, or meeting one-on-one with my own manager."

The group spent the next half hour discussing the finer points of the model and its impact on everyone involved in the conversation. Then they took a well-deserved coffee break.

Here is the CLEAR framework and some of those finer points (see Figure 8.2):

- **Connect:** People buy from people they like and trust. That's why *establishing rapport* is so critical to a successful conversation. It's not just happy talk; it's a skillful blend of connecting at both the professional and personal levels.

We remember a colleague—call him Thomas—who kept a Connections section in his notebook, dedicating a page to each person he met. He divided the page into two sections with a horizontal line. Each time he spoke to someone, he tried to learn something new about them—something they did, something they thought. He kept track of these bits of information, putting professional items on the top half of the page and personal items on the bottom half. "It's how I connect with people," he said. "I just look at someone's page before we meet. Connecting becomes easy."

In the first few minutes of a conversation, it's also important to agree on an agenda, the outcome you're after, and how much time you have to talk. These three things frame the conversation you're about to have. And, very importantly, it lets you know how much time you've got for the next step.

Spend approximately *half* of the conversation using the skill of *Precision Listening*.

- **Learn:** The "L" icon in the Figure is filled with a solid color. This is a reminder to spend approximately *half* of the conversation using the skill of *Precision Listening* illustrated in the story of John's training. Whether you're selling, managing, or collaborating with colleagues, learning more about *their* thinking is the key to stimulating your *own* thinking.

Take your time; follow their lead. Say, "tell me more" to help them go deeper. Learn something new so that you have something new to work with. Refuse to control the conversation. Follow your curiosity. Practice patience—you'll have time later to ask your questions and offer your thinking. *Split Attention is the key to doing this consistently and well.*

As Edward said, "linger longer" in this step. Then, about halfway through, move on to the next step, or you won't have enough time to create the committed action you're after.

> Learn something new so that you have something new to work with.

- **Educate:** When the time for Learning has run its course, ask for permission before you move to this stage: "Is there anything else you want me to hear before I share what I've been thinking about this?" Often there will be one more thing they want you to know or understand.

You'll be glad you waited until now to ask your questions and provide your input. You'll wind up saying less and having more impact. Be considerate and direct. It's their responsibility to decide what to do, but it's your responsibility to give them your best thinking.

Keep an eye on the time. Be sure you get through the final two steps.

- **Ask for action:** When you've done the Learn and Educate steps as thoroughly as time permits, it is natural and easy to raise the subject of a very next step. The other person needs to decide what to *do* in order to move this conversation into action.

Anything less than a free, clear choice won't actually happen, or it will happen badly.

You may have suggestions about what the next step needs to be. Be sure to ask for their ideas first, but don't be shy about offering your own. The aim here is to help the other person get Above-the-Line in their attitude and make a commitment they want to keep.

- **Resolve:** This step is an *autopilot check.* In its simplest form, you ask the other person to think for a moment about what might get in their way of completing their VNS on time. They will wake up to any conflicts or potential obstacles and adjust their next step accordingly. This simple step leads to a committed choice.

  Occasionally, the person you're speaking with just isn't ready to take a VNS. There's something blocking them—perhaps a client has an objection, or a direct report is struggling with a way forward. What you need to do is cycle back through CLEAR, returning to the "L" step to learn more about what's in their way and how to resolve it.

This conversational framework takes practice. You'll be surprised how quickly you get good at some steps while struggling with others. Don't sweat it. Keep practicing. It will pay off.

CONNECT personally and professionally
- Make introductions and establish rapport.
- Set the agenda and timeframe.
- Save half the time for the **Learn** step.

LEARN about the situation
- Use Precision Listening and replay.
- Resist the urge to jump in—keep listening.
- Use *"Tell me more"* to open up conversation.

EDUCATE appropriately
- Get permission to share your thinking.
- Share your input boldly to set up next actions.
- Discuss the subject collaboratively.

ASK for action
- Ask questions to test interest.
- Ask for their very next step.
- Provide two alternatives if possible.

RESOLVE any blocks or concerns
- Replay the block, use S/A, and ask for others.
- Use Precision Listening for each block.
- Resolve the biggest block and get the VNS.

Figure 8.2 CLEAR Conversation

Executive Summary

The *itch to pitch* is difficult to overcome. You can use the transformational skills of managing attitude and leading CLEAR conversations to calm this automatic behavior. You'll sell more and be happier doing it. When you give up pitching, pursuing, and persuading and focus instead on using CLEAR conversations to move your clients through their DQ stages, you'll find your clients will actually *want* to be with you. And when clients *want* to be with you, they trust you. Sales happen more often, on a greater scale, and with far fewer headaches.

And, utilizing CLEAR in your sales management conversations and in your collaboration with colleagues creates discussions in which you learn new things, place responsibility for action where it belongs, and never again leave a conversation without committed action in place.

Now let's look at the critical role that managers need to play in creating a sustainable and flourishing selling system.

CHAPTER 9

BUILD YOUR PEOPLE

You don't build a business—you build people—
and people build the business.
—Zig Ziglar

Everyone agrees that sales managers are responsible for the performance of their teams. What's far less clear is exactly *what* sales managers are supposed to do to make this performance happen. In a very real way, the art of sales management is even more of a black box than the art of selling.

You can see the black box in action by looking at how most sales managers are promoted into their roles. As one sales manager told us, "On Friday at 6 PM, I was the company's number one seller. On Monday morning at 8 AM, I was the sales manager. I must have missed the management training over the weekend! Seriously, they must have thought that my success in sales automatically qualified me to manage other salespeople. After one month on the job, I can tell you that it doesn't!"

As new sales managers painfully learn, *managing* requires an additional set of skills beyond what they needed as salespeople. This is *especially* true for managers who want to develop a high performing DQ Sales® team.

> **As new sales managers painfully learn, *managing* requires an additional set of skills beyond what they needed as salespeople.**

If you look at these skill sets through the lenses of the transformational formula, R=A+C+E, it is obvious that sales reps *and* their managers benefit from mastering the skills of focusing on the right Results (aiming), managing Attitude (using Split Attention to stay Above-the-Line), and conducting Competent conversations (using CLEAR to get to committed action). Now, as we look at Execution, we see the special and absolutely necessary role sales managers play in the development of a self-sustaining sales team.

THE EXECUTION CYCLE

Great sales managers know how to develop their team's ability to *execute*—to initiate and maintain a *transformative cycle* of activity as they work. They know what to look for and what to do at each point in this cycle to help their team members develop into high performers.

The Execution Cycle has three phases, each of which prepares you for the next (see Figure 9.1). *Aiming* your brain at the results you seek launches you into a state of activity that, when done in an Above-the-Line state of mind, results in a high level of naturally brilliant performance that has been called Flow.[xxiv] To ensure your Aim stays true and you remain in Flow, you need consistent and effective periods of time when you step back from activity, reflect on what's happened, and learn from it. These are the Build moments, and *they* are the moments sales managers live for. One of our clients, a terrific sales manager, often said, "I don't manage numbers, I develop people."

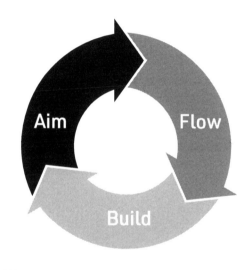

Figure 9.1 The Execution Cycle

If you're going to transform your sales force, you have to *first* transform your sales managers into competent *builders* of your sales reps. This requires structure, discipline, and a sustained willingness to learn—from everyone involved.

"I don't manage numbers, I develop people."

What does that look like?

A WEEK IN THE LIFE OF A SALES MANAGER

Transformative learning sometimes relies on *imagination* to create fresh neural pathways that put an end to automatic behavior and free us to make new choices. Imagining is another way to aim your brain, and it can generate flashes of insight about what's possible in your own situation.

So, right now, imagine you're a sales manager with a team of eight reps. You report to a sales director who manages five other people in your position. This is a highly effective director who has your back. You both attended the transformational training, and he has given you the green light to implement DQ selling and develop your team to succeed in it.

When you took the manager's training three weeks ago, you left knowing your very next step was to practice the transformational skills yourself, and you're getting the hang of it. Your awareness of your attitude is increasing, and you are using Split Attention more frequently during the day. You're aiming yourself thoughtfully on a weekly and daily basis, and you've survived your initial clumsiness with CLEAR conversations. You understand the specifics of your DQ selling system—the steps your clients must take, the actions your reps take to lead them through the process, and a simple tracking system to plan and record this activity.

Last week, you and your team completed the sales training. Early reports are enthusiastic, and together you're ready for your first full week of implementing what you've learned. You've got a plan, a structure to follow. You know you can't do it all perfectly, but you're going to give it your best. You remember a phrase from your training—"It's a mileage sport"—and you know you're in for the long haul.

You look at your plan for the week. You've carefully integrated into your schedule the preparation and the conversations you need to have with your salespeople to create the conditions in which they can keep *building* their sales capability. You've got the right meetings scheduled with your people, and you've received their Aim Plans for the week ahead. You've reviewed the pipeline and your team's very next steps with each of their clients. You've dumped your old team meeting format—that exercise in boredom and repetition—and you're ready for something new.

Monday

You start the weekly Sales Team Meeting by acknowledging last week's accomplishments. You mention by name each person who accomplished something significant—a

> You've dumped your old team meeting format—that exercise in boredom and repetition—and you're ready for something new.

sale, the movement of a deal from one DQ stage to the next, a personal victory over anxiety and hesitancy. You give a special acknowledgment to the two reps who showed up to an initial client meeting with only a notebook and a pen.

You ask Henri to share the details of how he got his client to calculate the cost of leaving their problems unsolved. You ask Lindsey to share how she gently but firmly refused to even discuss pricing until the client had signed off on the design for a solution that would solve the top five problems on their list.

You give the group a few minutes of Aim Time to review their plans for the week, eliminate distractions from their calendars, and ensure their next steps are scheduled at times they will be able to accomplish them. Then, everyone, including yourself, presents their Aim Plan for the week. You ensure they use the time well—clearly stating the specifics and their purpose for each objective, requesting what they need to succeed, and openly receiving everyone's suggestions and feedback on what they're planning to do. It's a lively conversation, and you're pleased to see several instances of cooperative activity that wouldn't have happened without this discussion.

When everyone has shared their plans, including you, you ask a direct question: "What might get in the way of you achieving your objectives this week?" The next few minutes are refreshing and constructive. There's no complaining, but there *is* honest discussion, along with analysis and suggestions about what has to happen for everyone to *win* this week. You discipline yourself to "praise in public and correct in private"— *not the reverse.*

At your direction, Ronald has prepared a short refresher on keeping attitude Above-the-Line. He walks the group through the exercise, and he receives a round of applause when he's done. You make the three announcements that the *entire* team needs to hear, and you finish the meeting early.

You have scheduled your client calls and company meetings to preserve a block of time in the afternoon to work with Erica. You've chosen her because, although she's not yet a top seller, she's closing in fast on that goal. She's a keen learner and worth this investment of your time.

You sit with her as she prepares for her client meeting. You watch what she does, and you ask her why she's doing it. You keep an eye on her attitude, and when you notice some uncertainty and struggle, you get her to acknowledge it. You take her through a brief exercise of splitting her attention and discussing what she really wants on this sales call. In a few minutes, she's back Above-the-Line and ready to go. You're getting good at this.

At the client meeting, you play your part and let her have the lead. When she makes mistakes, you split your attention and succeed in *not* jumping in to fix things. You're impressed when she works her way out of the problem. After the meeting, you listen carefully as she reflects on what happened. You offer your opinion and are pleased with her decision as to what she will do next time. She's on her way, and your time with her was well spent.

You finish the day on a high.

Tuesday and Wednesday

Over the next two days, you invest half your time observing the other team members who are ready for further development. You keep informal notes on your work with each person—what they're aiming at, their very next steps, what they do well, and what they struggle with. In every conversation, you learn something more about their thinking and behavior. You especially keep your eye on their attitude, and you actively intervene to help them stay Above-the-Line.

In these two days, you also begin your schedule of check-in calls with your team—a different weekly schedule with each person, depending on their clients, the state of their deals, their need to develop, and your need to know what's going on. Each call is unique according to the experience level of your direct reports and the complexity of the deals they are pursuing.

You keep the calls short, and you avoid long stories—either listening to them or telling them. You keep a sharp eye on their mindset, helping them raise their attitude when necessary. You focus on which DQ stages the clients have completed and your direct reports' next actions to move their clients forward.

Thursday and Friday

You continue your check-ins, sticking close to what's going on, putting out fires, and protecting your team from well-intended but misplaced demands from other people in the company. You are ruthless about your own schedule, letting nothing interfere with the times you've set aside to *build* your people's capacity to sell. A couple of your peers—in finance and marketing—are grumbling that you're not as available to meet as you used to be. But you know that building your team results in greater sales, and greater sales is what you're paid to deliver. It's how you buy your freedom to work as you please.

> You are ruthless about your own schedule, letting nothing interfere with the times you've set aside to *build* your people's capacity to sell.

You spend a few hours each day in one-to-one weekly review meetings with your direct reports. Together, you examine their activity of the past week—the tracking sheets they use to plan and record their selling activity, their actions to move clients through the DQ stages, their successes, and their failures. You are direct with your feedback and insistent on them practicing their new skills. You make sure they aim themselves wisely and well for the following week.

Also, you sit down with two of your team members for their monthly reflections. In these meetings, you avoid the details of their daily work. Instead, you focus their attention on the job itself—their satisfaction and fulfillment as they work, what they're learning, how they're growing, and the development they want in the following month. You can tell from this week's meetings with Erica and Nicholas that, when the time comes for the company's annual appraisal, you will already have done the heavy lifting.

Before you leave on Friday, you set your own plan for the following week. You are learning that you cannot *force* people to transform themselves and implement DQ selling. But you can *require them* to do the things by which they will *transform themselves* to sell in this new way.

You notice that the people who adopt these practices *want* to keep working in this way. You also notice the one person on your team who is strongly resisting the process. You have a calm conviction that, soon, either he will quit, or you'll let him go. It won't be a surprise. There's no need for him, or you, to be miserable. You're building a high-performing team of people who find this way of working exhilarating and rewarding, and you're keeping your eyes on the prize.

You leave work on time and head for home, family, and friends.

THE KEY PRACTICES

In this imaginary "week in the life" of a sales manager, we included some of the transformational practices our clients have found invaluable. They are simple and effective. Do them consistently and masterfully, and you will build self-motivating and self-correcting teams that transform their sales performance by focusing on the DQ of their clients.

The most important practice, of course, is to keep a watchful eye on *your own* attitude, your own state of mind, as you work. Maintain an Above-the-Line mindset that allows you to access your Deep Desire and the natural brilliance that brings out your best. Have CLEAR conversations with colleagues and clients that lift them Above-the-Line and generate committed action.

Then you need a structure of management activity—a series of regular engagements with your team members—in which you *require* them to transform themselves and *create the conditions* in which they can do so. Here's a list of those engagements—the practices you can use to build your people so they can build your business.[13]

> You need a structure of management activity—a series of regular engagements with your team members—in which you *require* them to transform themselves and *create the conditions* in which they can do so.

The Sales Team Meeting

A well-designed meeting starts the week (or the day) in a way everyone finds valuable. Recognize specific achievement, agree on plans for the coming week, identify and remove blocks to the success of these plans, refresh skills, and pass on information everyone needs to have.

---

13 Visit our website – www.wrpartnership.com – to find more specific information, downloadable models, and templates for these practices.

Don't use the sales meeting to review individual deals. Instead, focus on the *whole* team and getting them ready to go. You can meet in person or

Don't use the sales meeting to review individual deals.

remotely. But, if you're going to work with your team remotely, be sure to use video conferencing. It is *so* much more effective than voice only.

The Three Conversations

Highly effective sales managers have learned *not* to have the same conversation over and over again with their sales reps. They treat each team member as an individual, and they have three *distinct* kinds of interaction. In each conversation, they utilize the CLEAR framework and keep in mind all three elements of R=A+C+E: attitude, competence, and execution. And they make sure each conversation is WMT—*worth my time*—for everyone involved.

Check-ins last no more than 15 minutes, are often done by phone, and occur multiple times each week. Schedule them differently for each team member according to their level of experience and your need to know what's happening. These calls focus on tactics, exchanges of information, and quickly managing mindset to keep the salesperson in Flow. Done well, these calls greatly reduce interruptions, avoid delays, and address issues before they become crises.

Personal Conferences occur weekly, if possible, twice a month at a minimum. Take a full, uninterrupted hour for this one-on-one meeting. Review in detail what the salesperson aimed to do and what they actually did in the previous week.

Make sure each conversation is WMT— *worth my time*—for everyone involved.

Examine the progress of each deal through the DQ stages. Avoid the usual, narrow focus on the size of the deal and its closing date. Instead, ask four questions that give a fuller picture of what needs to happen to increase the client's decision intelligence.

1. "What DQ stage is your client at?"
2. "What *prior* stages have they not completed?"
3. "What stage are you leading them to next, and why?"
4. "What is your very next step to lead them forward?"

Acknowledge what they've done well, help them learn from their mistakes, and ensure they create an Aim Plan for the following week.

Professional Reflections happen monthly. In these meetings, *avoid* discussing the details of deals, strategies, and tactics. Instead, focus on the big picture. Have a 50,000-foot conversation about life and work.

Ask about the job itself, their level of fulfillment and personal satisfaction with what they do day-in and day-out. Explore their career aspirations and discover what you can do to help them succeed and advance. Focus their attention on the personal and professional development they want over the next 30 days and commit to the part you can play in it.

Invest your time and energy into the growth of your direct reports, and you will build a team that will walk over hot coals for you.

The Right Data

All three of these transformational conversations need to be based on *reality*—things that *actually* happened or failed to happen. Everything else is *story* and, to be blunt, *useless* for permanent change. So many man-

> Invest your time and energy into the growth of your direct reports, and you will build a team that will walk over hot coals for you.

agement conversations wander down roads to nowhere: explanations, excuses, insights, and suggestions that change little except the level of frustration felt by everyone involved.

Building a salesperson's ability to perform requires the right data—nothing extra—and data that is accurate and timely. For many sales managers, that's where the problem lies. They're *drowning* in data, most of which is inaccurate, outdated, and irrelevant to the task of developing their salespeople into high performers.

We've watched many companies invest huge amounts of money and effort into sophisticated software, hoping that the data it generates will improve the performance of their sales force. Usually, this doesn't work. Yes, there's more data—*lots* of it—but it's still inaccurate, outdated, and irrelevant!

There's a very interesting reason why this happens. A CRM produces an accurate forecast only when it is *first* used by the sales reps to *plan* their selling activity. Salespeople love to plan when it helps them succeed. They hate to report on things after the fact. They see it as busywork, and they'd rather talk to clients.

When companies use their CRMs effectively, the system becomes a sales *planning* tool that also produces forecasts and reports that are relevant, accurate, and valuable.

So, how do you transform your data-gathering processes if you're already awash in information you don't trust? Enroll your sales force to do two simple things, consistently, honestly, and completely.

- **Aim**—Everyone—reps and sales managers—writes an Aim Plan for the upcoming week. List your most important objectives, your purpose for achieving them, and the very next steps you are going to take to make each one happen. Schedule each VNS in your calendar.

  Start each day with some Aim Time. Review your Aim Plan, remove from your inbox and calendar *anything* that distracts or interferes with your aim. (Yes, there will be times when an interruption is unavoidable, but, if you're determined, you'll find those times are far less frequent than you imagine.) Fine-tune your schedule for the day, and stay on track with your Aim Plan.

- **Plan and track sales activity**—Everyone in charge of a deal—whether a sales rep or a sales manager—uses a Sales Activity Planner to *plan* and *track* their selling activity for every deal they are pursuing. At a glance, they can see which DQ stages their clients have completed and the very next steps they're taking to lead their clients forward.

  At first, do this on a simple spreadsheet. Later on, you can integrate the DQ stages into your company's CRM.

  Sales managers need to *create the conditions* that make it possible for sales reps to use this spreadsheet honestly and accurately. No more pressing reps to make unrealistic plans, no more demands for activity that tempt them to falsify their numbers.

People can transform their sales performance when they compare what they *aimed to do* with what they *actually did.* Doing this without story, excuse, or blame becomes a wake-up call that allows them to turn off their autopilot and turn on their brilliance.

Executive Summary

Execution is a virtuous loop of three fundamental activities: salespeople Aim themselves wisely, work in a state of Flow, and continue to Build their capacity to play their part in the development of your business.

Transformation requires leadership. This is the job of the sales manager. It requires support from above and a *structure* of engagement between manager and direct reports that empowers your sales reps to *execute* your selling system.

Your managers create the conditions for execution to flourish by conducting a transformed sales meeting and three types of one-to-one conversations, each with a distinct purpose. The data that makes these meetings work comes from a CRM your salespeople use as a *planning* tool to help them succeed.

YOUR VERY NEXT STEPS

Transformation doesn't run by the clock. It makes its own time, and you can learn to follow its progress and know when to make your next move. Start simply, learn as you go, and experiment with these steps at your own pace—depending on the nature of your company, the size and shape of your sales force, the complexity of your operations, and your position of influence within it.

> **Transformation doesn't run by the clock.**

Follow these four steps, and you'll be on your way.

1. Start with Yourself

You've probably heard Gandhi's advice on leadership: "Be the change you want to see." In the words of one of our mentors, "You can't lead where you won't go, you can't teach what you don't know."[xxv] Here are four practices to try out.

Over the next few days, start by paying attention to your state of mind. Notice when you're Above-the-Line and when you're Below-the-Line. Don't judge yourself; just watch your attitude rise and fall.

Also you can start practicing with Split Attention. Get to the point where you remember to do it several times a day. When you begin an activity, use the phrases "I want…and I want *that* because I want…" to discover the deeper desire that underlies what you're after.

Consciously follow the steps of a CLEAR conversation as you talk with colleagues and clients. Spend half your discussion *learning* what *they* think, want, or suggest. Ask for permission *before* offering your own opinions. Make sure the conversation concludes with committed actions.

Before you leave for the weekend, write an Aim Plan for the following week. Start each day with some quiet Aim Time to sharpen and focus on what you're going to do.

You'll know that you're ready for the next step when you notice changes in your thoughts and behavior *and* when people closest to you notice the changes as well. That's transformation at work. *Trust* this process; it will *equip* you to help others do it for themselves.

Trust this process; it will *equip* you to help others do it for themselves.

2. Watch What's Happening

Gather a few like-minded people and share what you're doing and why you're doing it. See if they want to join you on the transformational journey. Together, observe more closely your salespeople and your sales managers as they work. Keep track of what you notice them doing and ask them for the thinking behind their activity. Resist giving advice or suggestions—just keep observing and learning.

Use the R=A+C+E formula to organize your observations. Clarify the results people are seeking. Notice their attitude as they work—when it's up and when it's down. Assess their competence as they interact with others—which parts of CLEAR they do well, and which need more work. Pay close attention to *how* people sell and manage salespeople. What is the *real* selling system at work in your company, and what do people *actually* do to execute it? What is the *real* sales management structure that your managers employ, and what *actually* happens when they engage their direct reports?

Make a list of the problems you need to solve to transform your sales organization. Put them in priority order. You'll know this step is complete when you have a prioritized list and a written calculation of what it is costing your company to leave these problems unsolved. This is the foundation of your business case for change.

3. Experiment with the Best

Choose your best people—those who are high performers *and* great learners—and together design a pilot program in which you can develop a DQ selling system that's right for your clients. Develop the practices and structure that will support them to make the system work.

Then, try it out. Get the help you need to have a training in which this group can *experience* a transformed way of thinking and acting. Learn as you go, change to meet the challenges that emerge, stay the course, and measure the results—outputs *and* inputs.

You'll know this step is complete when you've got the results you want *and* the understanding of how you got them.

4. Roll It Out To the Rest

When you've got a selling system that works—that produces sales results *and* increased well-being for everyone involved—figure out how to roll it out to the rest of your sales force, starting with the people who are *most ready and able to change.*

One word of caution: Not everyone will welcome this activity with open arms. That's a *good* thing. Your program becomes a line in the sand—declaring what it takes to sell and to manage sales in *your* company. Within a month or two, you'll probably find that about half your sales force is really catching on, most of the rest are giving it a go but struggling with parts of the process, and a small percentage are opting out—quitting the process or quitting the company. You can trust *all* of these developments because they will get you where you want to go.

You'll know it's working when your sales force is committing instead of hedging, getting great instead of getting by, and staying on track instead of just staying busy. And the sales results will speak for themselves.

It's a great adventure. Go, make it happen.

THANK YOU

We'd be delighted to hear from you—your stories, feedback, or how we can support the sales transformation you want to lead.

You can reach us through our website:
www.wrpartnership.com or by writing us directly at
connect@wrpartnership.com

—Roy and Scott

ACKNOWLEDGMENTS

This book is a product of the working relationship we've enjoyed over 35 years. And that relationship has been influenced and informed by our many teachers, mentors, colleagues, and friends.

You know who you are, and we trust that you know the gratitude we feel for your contribution to our lives. We wouldn't be doing this and doing it in this way if it weren't for you.

With the certainty that we're leaving somebody out, and with our apologies for doing so, we recognize the following people who have especially contributed to the thinking and practices that have shaped this book: our Strategic Leadership Team and fellow consultants at WRP; our clients, many of whom have become friends; Nicole and her talented team at Niche Pressworks; and a special word of gratitude to our own COO, Jessica Gustafson, for her editorial expertise.

And, as always, we thank our families for creating a centered and strong "home" from which we could depart to do our work and to which we could return to be replenished.

ABOUT THE AUTHORS

W. Roy Whitten and Scott A. Roy are the co-founders of the international sales consultancy, Whitten & Roy Partnership. WRP maintains a global consultant network and has guided businesses and organizations in over 40 countries to transform the way they sell.

Roy Whitten is an expert in transformative learning and its role in sales performance. In 2004, he earned a Ph.D. for his work in transformative learning and change. In over 40 years as a trainer, consultant, and coach, he has personally supported the development of thousands of people throughout the world.

Scott Roy spent the first part of his career building and running large, direct-sales organizations. He co-founded a national insurance company that has grown to over $2B in assets. Since 2005, he has been a consultant and coach to companies throughout the world.

If you'd like more information about the authors or WRP's services, please visit their website: www.wrpartnership.com.

ENDNOTES

i   "Business Roundtable Redefines the Purpose of a Corporation to Promote 'An Economy That Serves All Americans,'" August 19, 2019. https://www.businessroundtable.org/business-roundtable-redefines-the-purpose-of-a-corporation-to-promote-an-economy-that-serves-all-americans.

ii   Eight months later, Peter S. Goodman wrote an article that illustrates the difficulty some of these companies are having implementing these visionary ideas: "Big Business Pledged Gentler Capitalism. It's Not Happening in a Pandemic." as published in the New York Times, April 13, 2020, https://www.nytimes.com/2020/04/13/business/business-roundtable-coronavirus.html?action=click&module=Well&pgtype=Homepage&section=Business.

iii   Matthew Dixon and Brent Adamson, *The Challenger Sale* (Penguin Group, 2011).

iv   "Talk About Value," citing research by Neil Rackham as published in *Forbes* magazine in June 2013, https://www.talkaboutvalue.com/blog/87-percent-of-training-knowledge-is-wasted-without-further-coaching-or-reinforcement-activity.

v   See the work of Jack Mezirow. Also, see the curriculum for Transformative Studies at places like the California Institite of Integral Studies, where Roy received his Ph.D. in 2004.

vi   The British philosopher, Alan Watts.

vii   This parable is attributed to G.I. Gurdjieff by authors P.D. Ouspensky, Charles T. Tart, and Jacob Needleman.

viii   Mack Hanan, *Consultative Selling: Seventh Edition* (New York: AMACOM, 2004).

ix   Jeffrey M. Schwartz, M.D. and Sharon Begley, *The Mind and the Brain: Neuroplasticity and the Power of Mental Force* (New York: Harper Collins ebooks, 2009), Kindle edition. Also see the work of cognitive researchers and therapists Albert Ellis and Aaron T. Beck.

x   See the work of neuroscientist Joseph E. LeDoux.

xi   *Oxford English Dictionary.*

xii   David Eagleman, *Incognito: The Secret Lives of the Brain* (New York: First Vintage Books, 2011), Kindle edition.

xiii   Proverb, often attributed to Idris Shah, Sufi author and teacher.

xiv   Lewis Carroll, *Alice's Adventures in Wonderland* (New York: Millennium Publications), Chapter VI.

xv   If you want help with this, we recommend the best book we've found on the subject: David Allen, *Getting Things Done: The Art of Stress-Free Productivity* (New York: Viking Penguin, 2001).

xvi   Maxwell Maltz, *Psycho-cybernetics: A New Way to Get More Living out of Life* (New York: Simon & Schuster, 1960).

xvii   The esoteric Russian philosopher, Gurdjieff, as recounted by his colleague, P.D. Ouspensky, *In Search of the Miraculous* (New York: Harcourt Brace Jovanovich, 1949), 14-15.

xviii   We acknowledge Dr. John Hoover who created this approach.

xix   Charles T. Tart, *Waking Up: Overcoming the Obstacles to Human Potential* (New Science Library, Shambala, 1987), ix.

xx   We are grateful for the pioneering work of our colleague and friend, Dr. John Hoover, who licensed us to incorporate his mapping of *Below-the-Line* attitudes into this model.

xxi   W. Roy Whitten, "Awake and Aware: the Practice of Split Attention in Everyday Life" (PhD diss., California Institute of Integral Studies, San Francisco, 2004. Split Attention is a variation of what Gurdjieff called self-remembrance and Ouspensky called divided attention.

xxii   Schwartz and Begley.

xxiii   We acknowledge David Allen for this concept.

xxiv   Mihaly Csikszentmihalyi, *Flow: The Psychology of Optimal Experience* (New York: Harper Perennial, 1990).

xxv   Bob Lightener, one of Scott's early mentors.

Printed in Great Britain
by Amazon

67325397R00104